THE PROBLEM WITH

THE PROBLEM WITH

Women in Ministry
Leadership

*An answer to those
who mistakenly believe that
women should not be spiritual leaders*

Commended to The Word
ctw Equipping Leaders
for Ministry Impact

Daniel A. Brown, PhD

UCLA

Jenifer A. Manginelli, MATS

GEORGE FOX

Kelly C. Tshibaka, JD

HARVARD

©*Commended to The Word*

~ to my young friends ~

As you have, likewise, been filled,

So get yourselves up on a high mountain

To preach, prophesy and lead,

While others of us begin to publish our dreams.

TABLE OF CONTENTS

Introduction

by Daniel A. Brown, PhD

W alking with God and coming to know His ways better and better is a journey. We're always on the way to His intended future for us, and that often means we're coming out of past practices and understandings. A shift in thinking, like a change in course, must come through the Holy Spirit's prompting—not as a result of strident debate or the insistence of others. As Paul encourages,

> "*Let us not judge one another anymore, but rather determine this—not to put an obstacle or a stumbling block in a brother's way...The faith which you have, have as your own conviction before God.*"
>
> ~ Romans 14:13, 22

In this book you will hear three voices, three expressions of personal conviction from individuals who believe God's intent is to mobilize all of His Church by endorsing both men and women for leadership roles. Each writer knows there are many complexities to this issue. Those complexities have given rise to new terminology, like *complementarian* and *egalitarian,* whose topic-specific definitions cannot yet be found in dictionaries read by our society.

The new words and the meanings behind them prove we do not yet understand everything about the topic. New words are to philosophers what Paris fashions are to retailers—a hint of what will one day be familiar to regular people. It will take some time before the words and their meanings in this debate migrate from academia to normal conversations in church. As yet, however, neither the ideas nor their labels are mainstream.

While some in the Church may wonder, *"What's the big deal? Can't we all just get along?"* However, those of us who wrestle with congregational leadership—and how to align the practices and structures of our corporate response to God's word—cannot escape the huge implications our beliefs have for others under our care. To the extent that church leaders embrace or resist *women-in-ministry-leadership*, the members of their churches will be encouraged toward or away from certain kinds of ministry activity.

> **The question of who is qualified (enough) and "called" into ministry leadership goes far beyond gender.**

Not all women want ministry leadership roles. That does not mean they are less spiritual or less committed than those who do. Among men, the same division of labor exists. God calls some to one aspect of ministry service; He calls some to other aspects. Nothing of what we've written should suggest that every woman or man ought to aspire to ministry leadership. We're simply talking about the option, the possibility, for Phoebes of the 21st century to emerge[1]—for women to have opportunity to be like their long-ago sister, Junia, who found Christ before Paul did, and was *"outstanding among the apostles."*[2]

The question of who is qualified (enough) and "called" into ministry leadership goes far beyond gender. Age, personal history, education, marital status, experience level and current lifestyle have long been part of the larger debate about who can and should lead Jesus' Church. What makes the question of gender unique within this discussion is the simple fact that gender isn't an optional aspect of someone's life. Individuals can change their lifestyle, choose not to marry, enroll in theological study, etc.

---

[1]Romans 16:1
[2]Romans 16:7

It is one thing to tell those who *"aspire to the office of an overseer"*[3] that in order to become (more) qualified and to prepare for church leadership, they should do or not do various things. It is quite another to dismiss any possibility of their leadership on the basis of their unchangeable *made-in-God's-image* being.

That is part of what makes this such a big question. Leaders' perspectives about its answer will shape what they say to their congregants—and what ministry they encourage. That ties in directly with believers' destiny, by mapping out some of the parameters for their life-long assignment and the subsequent evaluation we're all longing to hear when our life on earth is over *("Well done, good and faithful servant."*[4]). Sons and daughters of the Most High God live under the same injunction: *"Fulfill your ministry."*[5] The question for women is, does that "ministry" include leadership?

Among credible biblical scholars and theologians, opinions vary. Within congregations, sincere followers of Christ disagree. Even those pastors who advocate the doctrinal validity of female leaders put their theology into practice in different ways and to different degrees. For some believers, the role of women in the Church has become a litmus test—almost a deal-breaker—of the Church's willingness to reach into 21st Century culture. For others, it isn't much of an issue.

Why and how women should fit within the leadership of the Church is complicated—and not the sort of question that will likely be resolved for everyone in the same way. That's why the voices in this book are personal and nuanced. Our goal is to offer perspectives—from the whole of Scripture—that explain why many of us who love the Church and adhere diligently to the word of God, find no reason to limit women's role in ministry leadership.

This is not an academic paper suitable for journal publication; few scholarly sources are referenced. As lead writer, I accept personal

---

[3] 1 Timothy 3:1
[4] Matthew 25:21
[5] 2 Timothy 4:5; see also Colossians 4:17

responsibility for that decision, and I hope it will not be misconstrued as anti-academic—or as some absurd contention that we are better served in our discussion by uninformed and unsubstantiated opinions couched in religious, *"I-have-the-mind-of-Christ"* utterances.

Hopefully, this book will stir others to dialog. The Foursquare Church, like many other Pentecostal groups, needs to shake off its anti-intellectual tradition and our suspicion of scholarship. We desperately need a better articulated theology, a more studied apologetic for what we believe. In addition to—and perhaps even before—practical discussions about what our churches could look like if we embraced our spiritual, denominational genome, we need academic conversations that incorporate the best textual studies and scholarly writings from the larger believing community.

In the meantime, since my preparation for ministry leadership never included academic training in Theology or Biblical Studies, I offer what I can to our ongoing dialog. My course of schooling at the university angled more in the direction of literature and philosophy. I believe the Bible is much more than mere literature or philosophy, but I bring the investigative strengths of those disciplines with me when I read God's word to unearth answers and patterns for my *life-in-Christ* and for my philosophy of ministry.

Additionally, as a ministry leader charged with making disciples and mobilizing more shepherds for God's flock, I chose to invite a couple of my *just-getting-started-in-pastoring* friends to the table where much of their future is being debated. You will be impressed with these younger voices that are neither strident nor shrill.

For my wife and my daughters, I want the ambiguity settled.

Kelly Tshibaka and Jenifer (one 'n') Manginelli are great reminders about the point of the debate. Whether academically studious or emotionally impassioned, however grounded in principle or practice, in whatever ways articulated with language, new or old—this deliberation within our Movement profoundly impacts real people: daughters and wives and sisters like Hilary, Lorrel, Jennie, Lindsay, Katee, Lynn, Geri, Heidi, Juniece, Christen, Ana, Mariella, Sabrina, Christy, Susan, Karee, Stacy, Jessica, Priska, Jessie, Judy, and Pamela...

If we need more open debate, let's have it. If we simply need to publicly publish our stance, let's do it. For my wife and my daughters, I want the ambiguity settled. If not for other denominations, at least for ours, living out, as it is, the legacy of a woman who was in ministry leadership!

One in Christ Jesus

by Kelly C. Tshibaka, JD

WOMAN, INTERRUPTED

When I was 3 years old, I sat on my dad's knee and my parents told me that when I grew up, I could be anything I wanted to be. I believed them. It wasn't until I started my legal career that I encountered the realities of the infamous "glass ceiling" that women hit in every profession.

Similarly, when I came to know Jesus at 8 years old, I read that there is no longer male or female because we are all one in Him. You know what? I believed Him. And it wasn't until I started pastoring that I encountered the realities of the *stained glass ceiling* that women hit across His Church every day.

In my professional career, I have worked, along with thousands of other women, to challenge the glass ceiling that limits the full use of women's talents and gifts. I grew up in an all-American, blue collar family that was supportive of anything I aspired to do. After diligently applying myself throughout college, I was admitted to one of the top law schools in the nation—which only began to admit women in 1950.

After graduation, I moved to Washington, DC, and obtained a position at the Department of Justice, the most competitive legal organization in the country. Then I focused my career on national security law, a highly selective field that handles all issues related to the War on Terrorism. I've worked hard to be a woman, a mom, and a highly effective attorney. And I currently hold a senior position in the government, overseeing the programs and operations of several federal agencies.

In my day-to-day work, I am trusted to make decisions that affect the national security of our country. But in a ministry context, if I give a word from God or teach from the Bible, then I encounter great resistance. Like the man who told me he thought women preachers were about as unbiblical as homosexual preachers. Or the people who won't be a part of our church because we support women in leadership. Or the friends I've lost because I'm a female pastor.

> *It astounds me that in the secular world of law and politics, women generally have more freedom to exercise their gifts and abilities than in the Church.*

It astounds me that in the secular world of law and politics, women generally have more freedom to exercise their gifts and abilities than in the Church. And yet it's in Jesus that we are supposed to experience the greatest love, freedom, and unity. After all, it's for freedom that He set us free.[1] Our Christian sub-culture trails secular society in recognizing that gifts, abilities, and callings are not gender exclusive. In my experience, the *stained glass ceiling* is far more difficult to penetrate than the *secular glass ceiling.*

The Questions of My Heart

In Genesis, we find the account of the creation of man and woman: *"Let us make man in Our image, according to Our likeness...in the image of God He created him; male and female He created them."*[2] At the very outset of the story, this verse raises two fundamental questions:

---

[1]Galatians 5:1
[2]Genesis 1:26-27

❧ As a Christian woman, what does it mean for me to be an image-bearer of God?

❧ What are women—and, more specifically, what am I—created to be and called to do?

My heart's question for Jesus mirrors the one He once asked His disciples: *"Who do you say that I am?"*[3] I want answers found in the Bible, rather than in cultural (or sub-cultural) convention, modern philosophical trends, personal predilection, or agenda-driven *gender-ology*. It is not satisfying to root myself in "what everyone else thinks." Public opinion is capricious, as Jesus Himself noted.[4] I am not interested in building the foundations of my identity and my purpose on sand; I want to build them on the Rock.[5]

THE GOSPEL STORY IN A NUTSHELL

The Bible is a story. The story goes like this: God, who is three-in-one, created Adam, who was alone. From Adam's side, He then created Eve. Though they were two, they were joined together in marriage and became one flesh. There was perfect oneness—they were one with each other, and they were one with God. When they sinned, however, the oneness was broken. Rather than being united with God and with each other, they struggled perpetually with separation from (and disunity with) God and each other.

Then, in love, God sent His one and only Son to die for our sin and to eliminate the brokenness that came with it. Because of Jesus' sacrifice on the Cross, those who believe in Him will not perish, but will have everlasting life.

Consistent with the original storyline, our oneness with God and each other is restored. And, so, throughout the New Testament, we see the

---

[3]Matthew 16:15
[4]John 2:24-25

[5]My thinking on this topic was influenced in part by ideas shared at the Synergy 2010 Women's Conference by Carolyn Custis James and Dr. Scot McKnight, in particular.

origin of a common unity—or *comm-unity*—among believers. This is the community of believers to which we belong today, and this is the community of believers through whom God has chosen to continue His redemptive plan. Finally, the story ends with a promise of what is to come— eternal unity and oneness with God (and each other), and a new heaven and a new earth in which all that was lost to us in Eden will be restored.[6] In short, the Bible is a story of oneness *created,* oneness *destroyed,* and oneness *restored* by a love so compelling that it warranted the ultimate sacrifice.

> *"It is not good for the man to be alone; I will make him a helper suitable for him."*

Answers from the Beginning

The purpose, role, and identity of women can be found in the pages of this story. For example, in the beginning when Adam was alone, God said, *"It is not good for the man to be alone; I will make him a helper suitable for him."*[7] This verse, along with post resurrection chapters, shows us three things that were true about women at creation.

First, *"it is not good for man to be alone:"* it is good for man to be with woman, partnering together in unity as an anointed alliance. Women are designed to partner with men. It is not good for men to be opposed to, set against, or at odds with women, nor is it good for women to be independent, separated, or divided from men. Instead, they were designed for togetherness and unity. Whether it is multiplying by creating children or multiplying by creating disciples, women are designed to partner with men.

Second, the word *"suitable"* is translated as *"corresponding to."* In other words, women were created to be the exact counterpart of, or to be the same in meaning or effect, as men. They share jointly in their blessing from God and in their ability to be fruitful, multiply, fill the earth, subdue it, and rule over creation.[8] Women were intentionally created to be different from men, but not to put them at odds with one another. Rather, they were made in a manner perfectly suitable for "being together."

---

[6]Revelation 21:1, 5
[7]Genesis 2:18
[8]Genesis 1:28

This is consistent with two other parts of the creation story: women were made in the image of God and are intended to be His image-bearers, while none of the animals in all the world corresponded to Adam. By forming Eve out of Adam's own flesh, and by fashioning her in His image, God emphasized that she was created to live in unity with Adam, working alongside him in their shared calling.

Third, the word for "helper" in Hebrew is *ezer,* which means a "help," or "one who helps." This word is used throughout the Old Testament to describe God as a quick and powerful *Helper,*[9] a *Protector,*[10] a *Rescuer and Liberator,*[11] and a *Help and Shield.*[12] Understanding that God is our *ezer* is foundational to our relationship with Him. As the psalmist writes:

> *"I will lift up my eyes to the mountains; From where shall my help [ezer] come? My help [ezer] comes from the Lord, Who made heaven and earth."*
>
> ~ Psalm 121:1-2

However, that is not the way our word "helper" is commonly understood or interpreted today. In modern usage, "helper" carries with it the connotation of being a subordinate, as in "mommy's little helper," an aide, an assistant, or a supporter. All of these are valued and appreciated roles and functions, but they are nevertheless subject to and unequal to the person being helped.

These connotations do not exist in the original Hebrew, however. When God made Eve an *ezer* for Adam, He did not make her subordinate to Adam. After all, if an *ezer* were subordinate to the one being helped, then God would be subordinate to mankind each time He helps,

The whole reason we want or need an ezer is because the ezer is able to do things we are not able to do!

---

[9]Deuteronomy 33:26; Psalm 20:2; Psalm 33:20; Psalm 70:5

[10]Deuteronomy 33:29

[11]Exodus 18:4; Deuteronomy 33:7; Psalm 33:20

[12]Psalm 115:9, 10, 11; Psalm 146:5; Hosea 13:9; Psalm 124:8

protects, or delivers. The whole reason we want or need an *ezer* is because the *ezer* is able to do things we are not able to do!

For instance, women think differently than men, relate to women differently than men, and have experiences and struggles that are unique to being a woman (such as being a wife, a mom, or a working woman). As a result, women often are better able to meet other women in places of specific ministry need—like ministering to women who have lost a child, have been raped or abused, who are heart-broken by their singleness, who have suffered emotional wounds inflicted by other women, or who wrestle through the dynamics of mother-daughter relationships.

Moreover, each woman has unique, God-given competencies, skills, and spiritual gifts. Rather than assuming these talents are for burying in subordinated ministry roles, I think it's far more biblical to believe that God intends for these talents to be invested in whatever ministry context He places these women.[13] Could it be that God is just as intentional today about placing certain men and women together for ministry purposes as He was at placing Adam and Eve together? In other words, isn't it more consistent with the Gospel story to believe that God has brought certain women into certain ministries because they are exactly the *ezer* that is needed *"for...such a time as this?"* [14]

> *...the story of the creation of Eve establishes women as an ally for men...*

When we read into Scripture the connotations of our modern day understanding of the word "helper," we miss an essential component of God's purpose, role, and identity for women; and we introduce confusion into His story. The story of the creation of Eve provides no basis for believing that God designed women to be subordinate to men. It also provides no basis for believing that God designed women to be superior to men. Rather, it establishes women as an ally for men—an ally that strengthens and complements men so well

---

[13]Matthew 25:14–30
[14]Esther 4:14

that *together,* and with God's help, they *will* prevail over any enemy or adverse circumstance they face.[15]

In essence, the story of Eve's creation reveals God's plan and design for man and woman to be one with Him and with each other.

WOMEN AND THE STORY

Because of sin, the intended anointed alliance between man and woman was destroyed. They no longer operated in unity and as one. Instead, the Bible recounts story after story of disunity and division between man and woman. Laban used his daughter as a pawn to extort seven years of service from Jacob. Naomi and Ruth were left destitute because they had no societal worth apart from the men in their family. Abraham conspired with Sarah to commandeer Hagar's womb. In short, sin birthed a cultural and societal framework in which women generally were subordinated to men in every way.

> *All of the divisions between people that served to subordinate one to another no longer exist in Christ.*

But Jesus ushered in a new order. Everyone who is in Christ is a new creation.[16] The old way of doing things—the broken oneness between people—is gone, and the new has come. All of the divisions between people that served to subordinate one to another no longer exist in Christ.

Then, after Jesus' resurrection, the Bible recounts an increasing release of spiritual gifting, power, and ministry among women in this new (or restored) order. Jesus used women as the first evangelists and the first witnesses to His glorious resurrection; the female disciples received the power of the Holy Spirit at Pentecost, along with the men; and, women like the first century apostle, Junia, were appointed by God to spread the Gospel and build His Church.[17] Jesus restored the intended framework for relationship between and among all His children, including men and

---

[15]Deuteronomy 33:29; Psalm 146:5; Psalm 124:8
[16]Galatians 6:15
[17]Matthew 28:5-8; John 20:18; Acts 1:14; Acts 2:17-18; Romans 16:7

women. We see the early Church living out the words written by the apostle Paul: *"There is neither Jew nor Greek, there is neither slave nor free man, there is neither male nor female; for [we] are all one in Christ Jesus."*[18]

Nevertheless, the redemption story is not fundamentally about women's liberation (at least, not in the social or political sense of the term). But we still can glean answers from it about what women were created to be and called to do, and about what it means for women to be image-bearers of the Living God.

> *I have found that when I am firmly rooted in God's purpose, call, and promises, I am more effective at ministering the love of Christ than when I lose sight of them.*

I have found that when I am firmly rooted in God's purpose, call, and promises, I am more effective at ministering the love of Christ than when I lose sight of them. Just as Peter began sinking in the waves when he lost sight of Jesus, I, too, find myself sinking in a storm—a storm of cultural pressures and implicit expectations—when I lose sight of who I am in Christ.

When this happens, I start to doubt myself. I get afraid. I pull back from ministry, and I hold back the truth and love of God. I allow myself only to perform administrative or children's ministry roles (universally acceptable for women), and I table my other gifts. I lament the gifts God has given me because it hurts so much that I don't get to use them. I become angry, insecure, and defensive. And I also check out (my passive version of quitting).

On top of all that, tensions arise in my marriage and in our ministry. I let my husband down as he begins to shoulder our ministry responsibility himself, and I leave him out there alone to shepherd people and battle the enemy. He can become frustrated with me, and our "lack of oneness" can become palpable. Which all makes sense—I'm not being the *ezer* he needs me to be (or that God intended me to be).

---

[18]Galatians 3:28

The Hard Parts

Working through these storms has forced me to wrestle with some difficult questions about God's purpose and calling for women. I've searched for answers to help me apply the Gospel story to my life today. For instance:

- Are women allowed to hold any ministry positions? If so, what kinds of ministry positions can they hold?

- Can they hold ministry *leadership* positions, such as the office of a pastor or teacher, for example?

- What about the verses in the New Testament that say women are to remain silent, women cannot teach or have authority over men, and wives must submit to their husbands?

The following article by my mentor and friend, Daniel Brown, addresses many of these issues in detail. Taking a Bible-based approach, Dr. Brown unpacks controversial passages of Scripture, and shows how they can be read consistently with the Gospel story. His reflections are not intended to be textbook arguments, but rather to serve as a discourse

> *...certain passages of Scripture...can only be interpreted one way when read in light of the totality of Scripture and the whole of the Gospel story.*

for practical application. He shows that, while certain passages of Scripture can be interpreted multiple ways when taken in isolation and out of context, they can only be interpreted one way when read in light of the totality of Scripture and the whole of the Gospel story.

Knowing and understanding what the Bible says about *women-in-ministry-leadership* is only part of the challenge we face. The other part of the challenge is figuring out how women can live out their identity in Christ in a church culture that often is opposed to appointing women as ministry leaders.

- How can women who are confident in their calling respond to those who have overlooked, belittled, demeaned, or hurt them?

❧ How can men who support *women-in-ministry-leadership* respond to those who challenge their position in a hostile or divisive way?

The final chapter in this book, by Jenifer Manginelli, addresses how believers can apply the truth of the Gospel Story in their individual contexts. Using biblical examples, and sharing from personal experience, she offers a godly way of thinking about how to engage individuals who oppose *women-in-ministry-leadership*, and how to function in environments that are hostile to the appointment of women as ministry leaders.

I see the objective of this book as two-fold:

1. To provide an explanation, drawn from Scripture and based on the Gospel Story, for why ministry leadership should not be determined by an individual's gender, any more than it should by the person's social status or race; and,

2. To offer perspectives on how women can function in their calling while being at peace with those who do not support *women-in-ministry-leadership*.

My position is not a compromise or an accommodation to current trends. Rather it is heart-felt obedience to what we believe the Bible commands. We seek to release spiritual ministry, not to platform gender; we long to humbly shepherd believers toward possibilities for serving Christ, not to create divisions between believers who hold differing opinions on this issue. My prayer is that in this book you will find answers to your questions—answers that will bring you into greater unity and oneness with God and His Church.

The Problem With
The Problem

by Daniel A. Brown, PhD

The student-led campus ministry I joined in college was completely gender-blind. Perhaps because the needs were so great, and the workers few, the only question we ever thought to ask was whose schedule of classes enabled them to lead a Bible study, staff the literature table on Bruin walk, or liaison with other Christian ministries at a quarterly meeting.

I suspect another reason for our lack of concern about who led what was our informal, unofficial status. We were *para*-church—a group, an organization, a chapter, etc. As such, we were likely absolved from the rules and conventions that govern "real" churches. After all, a Bible study or a monthly praise gathering aren't really churches—are they?

So, my earliest response to women (students) in ministry leadership was, *"Great. Glad you're available. We need you!"* Frankly, I was unaware of the debate about their place in the Church—and what my co-laborers in college would be allowed to do after they graduated into the real church world. Some of my friends came from church traditions that disallowed *women-in-ministry-leadership.* It was strange for me to witness these friends, several years later, when they were relegated to diminished leadership roles compared to what they enjoyed—and were able to do—while in college.

Their increased maturity notwithstanding, they were no longer welcomed to contribute in the same way in *church-outside-the-college-bubble.* Unless, of course, they became missionaries, and led in other nations what they were not supposed to lead in ours.

My personal passion in those days—and ever since—was to lead Bible studies. I started a new Bible study each quarter for all of my undergraduate years, and most of my graduate studies. I was and am earnest about the Bible's unique power to transform lives. In it, and it alone, God reveals His ways. As an avid *student-of-the-Bible,* I made inquiry in its pages, looking for what it, in its entirety, teaches.

My preferred method of Bible study is simply to compile all verses and passages relevant to a topic, then examine each verse in its context to see how it fits with the other verses and passages. Piecing them all together informs my thinking on a subject. It's a simple process, but it has been profoundly helpful to me—and to others.

What follows in these pages is my Bible study on the topic of *women-in-ministry-leadership.* I have gleaned it from reading the Book, and it is not informed or shaped by having read any outside source—except for referencing the meanings of a few words in their original language. Some of my theologically educated friends made helpful suggestions and gave me some pointers along the way. But I have always preferred to work directly with the Bible *text-as-we-have-it,* reading and rereading it until it makes sense in my heart.

This is what I believe the Bible teaches about *women-in-ministry-leadership*—and how I interpret God's plan for us. I offer it to you as a pastor, not as a scholar.

A BIBLICAL OVERVIEW

> *"Then God said, 'Let Us make man in Our image, according to Our likeness; and let them rule...' God*

> *created man in His own image, in the image of God He
> created him; male and female He created them."*
>
> ~ Genesis 1:26-27

In the *"creative order,"* God shaped humankind in His image. He began with Adam, but unlike the other forms of life that God created in the beginning, Adam was unable to bring forth fruit after his *"own kind."* Without a partner, Adam alone was *"not good"* because he could not reproduce. Since *"all flesh is not the same flesh,"* God fashioned Eve from the self-same flesh of Adam. When Adam first beheld Eve, he cried out in self-recognition, *"Bone of my bone; flesh of my flesh!"* [1]

Eve was made of the same stuff as Adam, but they were not identical. God gave Eve a slightly different shape, so she would be an exact counterpart to Adam. They complimented each other perfectly. In a sense, they were like "left and right," or "in and out." God designed them to be together. The one (Adam) became two (Adam and Eve), so they could *"become one flesh"* [2] to produce life. That was God's original plan.

The physical "fit" was an essential part of His assignment for them to *"be fruitful and multiply and fill the earth."* [3] However, it was not the only connection God gave Adam and Eve. He also "fitted" them with shared dominion over the earth [4]—joint-rule over a creation that effortlessly yielded its *fruit-with-seed* for them. [5] Coming together as one, they were able to reproduce and rule. They were co-heirs, peers in partnership. They were equal but different, different but equal. Adam wasn't *over* Eve. Instead, they were *two-but-one,* a two-sided whole, *"male and female."* [6]

Adam and Eve's sin disrupted Creation on every front. Everything was thrown off the original plan. Many terrible, terrible consequences followed after their sin. The sin-force rushed into our world like flood-waters past a broken levee. Death punctured the life God wanted for us, and forever

---

[1] Genesis 2:23

[2] Genesis 2:24

[3] Genesis 1:28

[4] Genesis 1:26-28; Matthew 19:4

[5] Genesis 1:28-30

[6] Genesis 1:27

> *Adam and Eve still had a mutually-held, God-given purpose on earth—being fruitful and having dominion.*

changed Adam and Eve's relationship with God and Creation. But it did not nullify His assignment for them. Adam and Eve still had a mutually-held, God-given purpose on earth—being fruitful and having dominion.

In the aftermath of sin's destruction, however, fulfilling that assignment was going to be more difficult. Children would be born to Eve in *'itsâbôn (labor, sorrow, pain);* crops would be cultivated by Adam in sweat and *'itsâbôn (labor, sorrow, pain).*[7] The fruit of both flesh and field required harder work from that point on. Nevertheless, their calling remained the same as in the beginning, and God continued to carry out His original intent for our race—even after the Fall.

The Redemptive Order

As we already discussed, God's original plan required Adam *and* Eve—together as partners, as parents, as co-bearers of His image. The way in which Adam and Eve "fit" together in the decision process that led to sin wasn't good. Instead of being together to resist the Serpent's lies, they were separated from one another, and were deceived one at a time.

Sin changed the creative order. Adam and Eve messed things up terribly. That's why God also made changes—to redeem His purposes for His people on earth. We might call this the *"redemptive order."* Unfortunately, it is difficult to see just how redemptive God's *after-sin* plan truly was because we bundle everything God said and did together under one heading—the Curse. Yes, the Serpent was cursed. So was the ground. But God didn't damn Adam and Eve. He still loved them and wanted to provide for them, despite the calamity brought on by their sin.

It is quite interesting to view God's words to Adam and Eve in light of the "good" He still wanted to do for them—and to get them back together in the best way possible in such a fractured world.

---

[7]Genesis 3:16-19

Redemptive Provision and Equality

In addition to the obvious disadvantages that came to Adam and Eve, there are still some elements that clearly show God's plan for fulfilling His original purpose. For instance, *after* the Curse, God *"made garments of skin…and clothed them."*[8] In the creative order, they had no awareness of their nakedness;[9] in the redemptive order, God covers their shame! No one would say that clothes are part of the Curse. Instead, they are an expression of God's continued love—and eagerness to redeem the consequences.

Likewise, in the original arrangement, God *"brought"* Eve to Adam.[10] Adam had a completely untutored response to what he saw. He wanted her. Eve did not need to pursue Adam because he had all the motive and momentum necessary to "fit" with his *"helpmeet"* as one flesh. He would pursue her to the ends of the earth:

> *"For this reason a man shall leave his father and his mother, and be joined to his wife; and they shall become one flesh."*
>
> ~ Genesis 2:24

In the redemptive order, God brings Eve to Adam in a different manner. Though the Curse decreed pain in bearing children, God tells Eve, *"…your desire will [still] be for your husband."*[11] Without this provision, the pain of bearing children would likely have ended our race. God gave Eve a newfound desire to pursue Adam, even though the fruit of their togetherness would be born in pain.

I believe that the "rulership" role God assigned to Adam was like the kind of leadership Jesus exhibited. As Lord, Jesus served and shepherded His People.

---

[8]Genesis 3:21
[9]Genesis 2:25
[10]Genesis 2:22
[11]Genesis 3:16

God did something similar to Adam, altering the original design for his relationship with Eve. In the creative order, Eve was a *"helpmeet"* to Adam, someone who would protect, aid, succor and relieve him. In our vernacular, she "had his back." In the redemptive order, however, God gives Adam an augmented assignment *to rule (mâshal)* Eve. The Hebrew word *mâshal* isn't necessarily a domineering rulership, as readers tend to imagine. It's the same word that describes the place that the sun, moon and stars have in *governing "the day and the night."* [12] It has a stewarding connotation—as in taking care of things—like Abraham's oldest servant *"had charge of all that [Abraham] owned."* [13]

I believe that the rulership role God assigned to Adam was like the kind of leadership Jesus exhibited. As Lord, Jesus served and shepherded His people. He was not, at all, like the *"rulers of the Gentiles who lord it over"* people. [14] It is unimaginable that God would tell the first husband something different than He tells all husbands in the New Testament—that is, to love their wives *"as Christ also loved the church and gave Himself up for her."* [15] This rulership of Jesus in all of our lives is cause for celebration, not dread. So it was to be for Eve—and her daughters centuries later.

> **The whole point of two genders has always been one race connected together for shared fruitfulness and leadership.**

Though it makes him sound peevish, Adam would likely have dropped the whole connection with Eve once he saw it would be "work" to maintain it. Adam's charge was to consider his wife's needs [16]—and to meet those needs—not just see to his own. God assigned man a leadership function vis-à-vis his wife as a means of reinstating the original partnership they enjoyed in the creative order.

---

[12]Genesis 1:18
[13]Genesis 24:2
[14]Matthew 20:25-28
[15]Ephesians 5:25ff
[16]Genesis 3:16

16

The husband's responsibility to reorder his priorities toward servant-leadership in marriage, and the wife's responsibility to reorient herself to his headship, is not a statement of men over women in general—or of one gender without the other in ministry. The redemptive order was different from the creative order in pattern, but not in purpose. The whole point of two genders has always been one race connected together for shared fruitfulness *and* leadership.

Sin has not altered the fundamental equality of men and women. Both bear the image of God and both are being changed from glory to glory in the image of Christ. Since the woman's seed was that which would eventually produce Messiah and overcome the Serpent, there is no reason to imagine that God's rearrangements after the entry of sin into the world diminished her person or giftedness in ministry.

BIBLICAL MODELS OF MINISTRY LEADERSHIP

In the earliest account of man and woman in the Bible, we find partnership. That is not, in itself, a persuasive argument for the role of *women-in-ministry-leadership*. But it is a compelling precedent. A brief scan through the Bible reveals several particular women whom God used to teach, lead and supervise His people. From Genesis to Revelation, women have had roles of ministry leadership:

Old Testament

1. Miriam was called *"the prophetess,"*[17] and she was one of the three main leaders *"sent before"* Israel by God to take the people out of Egypt.[18]

2. Deborah, the wife of Lappidoth, sat as judge of Israel, keeping the land *"undisturbed for forty years;"*[19] her male assistant, Barak, deferred to her primary leadership role because he recognized her gifting/calling.

---

[17]Exodus 15:20
[18]Micah 6:4
[19]Judges 4:4–5; 5:31

3. When Hilkiah, the high priest, found the lost Book of the Law in 621 B.C., King Josiah chose to inquire of the Lord from the prophetess Huldah, *wife* of Shallum, who then prophesied to the high priest and to Josiah, the king.[20]

4. Esther used her royal powers to effect deliverance for her people, and Mordecai did according to what she commanded him to do.[21]

New Testament

1. After Peter and the rest of the (male) disciples denied Jesus and deserted Him, it is the women from amongst them "who come first to the tomb, who are the first to see the risen Jesus, and are the first to be entrusted with the news that He has been raised from the dead. This is of incalculable significance."[22]

2. On Pentecost, Peter reminded everyone that prophetic ministry and the outpouring of God's Spirit were promised to *"sons and daughters,"* old and young alike—all the bondservants of the Lord, *"male and female."*[23] That very day in the upper room, both women and men were filled with the Holy Spirit.[24]

3. Priscilla, who in an atypical manner is usually mentioned before her husband, Aquila, collaborated with him in teaching and correcting the understanding of eloquent Apollos, a man *"mighty in the Scriptures."*[25] As *"fellow workers"* with Paul, they co-pastored a church in their home.[26]

---

[20] 2 Kings 22:14–20

[21] Esther 4:13–17

[22] N.T. Wright, *"Women's Service in the Church: The Biblical Basis,"* a conference paper for the Symposium, 'Men, Women and the Church,' St John's College (Durham, September 4, 2004).

[23] Joel 2:28–29; Acts 2:17–18

[24] Acts 1:14; 2:4

[25] Acts 18:24–26

[26] Romans 16:3–5

4. When Saul ravaged the Church by *"entering house after house,"* men *and* women were put in prison or *"scattered throughout the regions,"* where they continued preaching the word.[27]

5. Philip, who was known as an evangelist, had four single daughters who were called *"prophetesses"* in the same way that Agabus was named a *"prophet".*[28]

> *At the time of Jesus' earthly ministry, the inclusion of women in significant spiritual roles would have seemed alarmingly radical. That did not matter to Him.*

6. Junia, along with Andronicus, was part of a prominent team of apostles.[29]

7. Phoebe was a deaconess *(diakonon)* of the church at Cenchreae,[30] as well as a benefactress *(prostatis)* of Paul.[31]

8. Various others, such as Nympha[32] and *"the chosen lady,"*[33] led churches.

EARLY DISCIPLES

At the time of Jesus' earthly ministry, the inclusion of women in significant spiritual roles would have seemed alarmingly radical. That did not matter to Him. Jesus regularly crossed the cultural and religious divides of His day. He healed *lepers,*[34] drew *children* to Himself,[35] welcomed *prostitutes* and *tax collectors,* exposed the barrenness of religious tradition[36] and spoke to *Samaritan women.*[37] He did not confirm religious convention or thinking.

It is true that the first twelve, named "disciples" were only men.[38] Jesus did not designate any women as apostles during His earthly ministry,[39]

---

[27]Acts 8:1-4
[28]Acts 21:8-9
[29]Romans 16:7
[30]Romans 16:1
[31]Romans 16:2
[32]Colossians 4:15
[33]2 John 1
[34]Luke 5:12-14
[35]Mark 10:14
[36]Mark 7:1-13
[37]John 4:7-38
[38]Matthew 10:1-4
[39]Luke 6:13

but, as mentioned earlier, Junia, a woman, is called *"outstanding among the apostles"* in Paul's letter to the Romans.[40] Jesus' selection of twelve men as founding apostles is no more a statement regarding gender qualification for ministry office (i.e., *men* only), than is the fact that the first to tell others about Jesus' resurrection were all women. Would we want to say that only women may tell of Jesus' resurrection?

While Jesus entered human history at a particular point in time, no one would suggest that we who were not alive in that era should be excluded from leadership in His Church! A snapshot from the beginning of His earthly ministry is not a complete picture of what Jesus' ministry has become over time. His roving band of twelve disciples included no 19th century Frenchmen, no 4th century women from the Balkans. But, as His followers grew in number over the centuries, His retinue encompassed every manner of people.

> *He wants His people to be a joined-together people, each of whom supplies meaningful ministry to the whole body.*

Remember, too, that the apostles were all Jews; however, no one insists that church leaders today must be Jewish. Because Jesus came to a particular place in the world, His followers were, initially, from that place only. They were Jews, the inheritors of God's promises. But He came for all people of all nations, and that is why we celebrate believers and leaders from every nation who belong to His Church. He includes all people based on faith: *"The gospel is the power of God for salvation to everyone who believes."*[41]

Those who identify themselves with Christ are united into a *"chosen race, a royal priesthood, a holy nation."*[42] In order to bond us together, God removes economic, religious, cultural and ethnic distinctions, as well as all other particulars of what we are *"according to the flesh."*[43] He wants *His* people to be a *joined-together* people, each of whom supplies meaningful ministry to the whole body.[44] That's why Paul tells all believers—not just

[40]Romans 16:7
[41]Romans 1:16
[42]1 Peter 2:9
[43]2 Corinthians 5:16
[44]Ephesians 4:16

men—to *"desire earnestly spiritual gifts, but especially that [they] may prophesy."*[45] The goal is that when the church gets together, *"each one has a psalm, has a teaching, has a revelation…"*[46]

That's how it was at the birth of the church on Pentecost. The *"tongues of fire rested on each one"* in the Upper Room,[47] and among those who gathered with the eleven disciples were certain *"women, and Mary the mother of Jesus"* (and His brothers).[48] Those women were also part of the ministry spill-over, *"speaking as the Spirit was giving them utterance,"* that enabled people of all languages to hear of *"the mighty deeds of God"* in their own languages.[49]

From the Upper Room

It was not just the men from the Upper Room who went into the marketplace. The women engaged, fully and equally, in that first ministry outreach. Their participation explains why Peter quoted from the prophet Joel about *"sons and daughters"* prophesying, and God's Spirit being poured forth upon *"both men and women,"* so that all mankind will have opportunity to call on the Name of the Lord.[50]

In the end, the great multitude in Heaven will come from *"every nation and all tribes and peoples and tongues,"* and they will stand *"before the throne and before the Lamb, clothed in white robes."*[51] But that scene of all peoples isn't the way Jesus' ministry started. He started with a few Jews and *"added to their number day by day,"*[52] including an Ethiopian eunuch,[53] a pharisaical persecutor of the church,[54] a Roman centurion with his friends and family,[55] and—eventually—the entire Gentile world.

> **Sometimes, limiting or restrictive practices can become confused with orthodoxy.**

---

[45] 1 Corinthians 14:1
[46] 1 Corinthians 14:26
[47] Acts 2:3
[48] Acts 1:14

[49] Acts 2:4ff
[50] Acts 2:17-18
[51] Revelation 7:9
[52] Acts 2:47

[53] Acts 8:25ff
[54] Acts 9:1-19
[55] Acts 10:1ff

The early Church was taken aback that God gave the Gentiles *"the same gift"* that He had given to them.[56] Ultimately, though, they realized that they would be *"standing in God's way"* if they held to their traditional exclusion of the uncircumcised.[57] Sometimes, limiting or restrictive practices can become confused with orthodoxy. The religious establishment—especially those with vested authority to teach—can, too easily, morph a liberating message into suppressive tenets. Historically, the place of women in the leadership of the Church seems reminiscent of that divisive exclusivity.

Just as the Gentiles are *"fellow heirs"* with the Jews through the gospel,[58] so, too, are women. Redeemed, anointed, gifted, called and loved by God in exactly the same way as men, women should be fully released to exercise their gifts in every facet of ministry in His Church. Though clearly out of sync with the culture at that time, men and women in the New Testament served in mutual, egalitarian ministry. Meaningful ministry in church was not limited to one gender, to one nationality, or to one age group.

> *Men and women are counterparts, and it serves no godly purpose for either gender to function autonomously, acting independently, without need of the other.*

Men and women are counterparts, and it serves no godly purpose for either gender to function autonomously, acting independently, without need of the other.[59] Making distinctions among ourselves for treating one group differently from another strikes me as less than God's intent. There is no place in the Church for biased treatment of people based on economic standing, racial heritage, national identity, political persuasion, religious upbringing or physical age; neither should there be discrimination on the basis of gender.

The qualification for ministry is not gender, but surrender.

---

[56]Acts 11:17; 15:7-11
[57]Acts 11:15-18
[58]Ephesians 3:6
[59]1 Corinthians 11:11

POSTURE OF SUBMISSION

In discussions like the one we're having about the appropriate role for *women-in-ministry-leadership,* there are usually several corollary issues that must be looked at because they influence our thinking—often in unconscious ways. For instance, in my college days we spent hours in discussion about God's will for our lives. The question was, how radically would we follow it? How much would we surrender to follow it?

Good questions! There is an obvious and correct answer to both. But many of us struggled to surrender because "God's will" had a connotation, a flavor, an implied meaning. Although no one ever taught me this, I somehow equated doing God's will with doing the things in life I least wanted to do! If I submitted to His plan for my life, I would be bored, unhappy and miserable—as a "good" Christian. My thinking was backwards, but I didn't know it.

Spiritual surrender (i.e. submission) is one of those side-issues that makes informed debate about *women-in-ministry-leadership* a bit more complicated because we are misinformed and misled about what it entails. For example, many people mistakenly associate several *negative-feeling* words with the whole concept of submission: *unthinking; servile; compliant; subservient; deferential to someone "better"; passive; inferior; silent; docile; etc.* Being *submitted* feels like the opposite of being *confident, visionary, firm, assertive, independent* and *self-sufficient.* Weaker people submit to stronger ones.

Fitting In

The Greek words usually translated *"to submit"* are closely related to one another: *hupeikō* means *to yield beneath, among, etc.; hupotassō* means *to arrange in an orderly manner beneath, among, etc.* In both cases, the primary idea is *fitting in with,* or *lining up with* someone or something else. Unfortunately, we instantly think of a hierarchy, an over/under relationship between a superior/inferior. The submitted one is presumed less valuable, less worthy, less qualified, etc.

ical view of submission clouds our discussion because
to" becomes synonymous with *"being less than."* We'll
biblical concept of submission more accurately if we think
of submission as *"fitting in with"* rather than just *"coming under"*
something or someone else. The purpose for submission is relationship
and connection. The two must correspond with each other like a bolt and
a nut: the nut's internal threads correspond with the bolt's external
threads. In order to fasten, they must submit to—fit in with—each other.
It is silly to ask which is greater, the nut or the bolt. Neither is much
without the other.

Submission may be hierarchical (above/below), but such a vertical
connection is not the only kind of submission. The relationship between
two things can just as easily be horizontal or mutual. For instance, we are
told to *"be subject (hupotassō) to one another,"*[60] and be subject to everyone
who *"helps in the work and labors"* or who has *"devoted themselves to
ministry to the saints."*[61] Submission can even take place within oneself:
the spirits of prophets are subject to prophets."[62]

For our topic of discussion, the most relevant form of submission is not
hierarchical (above/below), but sequential (first/second). One obvious
example of sequential submission is the alphabet. Things have an order to
them, but one "place" in the sequence is no greater than another. The
letters of the alphabet are *submitted* to one another in this manner. The
letters proceed from "A" and continue in right alignment to "B," "C,"
"D," etc. No letter is inferior to another—or less necessary. Even though
"D" is before "E," it isn't better.

And let us not forget the primary point for letters. They are used to spell
words and communicate ideas. Their "job" is not merely to keep
themselves in lined order. Yes, "P" does "follow" "O" and should stay
where kindergartners can memorize it in sequence. But its destiny is not
so paltry as just being *submitted!* It has a *submitted* place in the alphabet,

[60]Ephesians 5:21
[61]1 Corinthians 16:15-16
[62]1 Corinthians 14:32

but its true service to the world is to be used in various combinations with other letters to spell things out for people. Potentially, "P" positioned prior to "O" can point to positive and potent possibilities.

The alphabet starts with "A." There must be a "first" in a sequence, and we *submit* ourselves when someone else is the starting point—or, at least, prior to us in the order. That is one reason why Jesus is so often referred to as the *Firstborn…"of all creation,"[63] "from the dead,"[64]* and *"into the world."[65]* As believers who submit to Him, we are called the *"church of the firstborn."[66]* Jesus is first. We follow Him.

> **The point of submission is getting things to fit together harmoniously.**

The essence of *submission* is *following after* and *coming behind*—but not for the convenience of others to leave us behind or leave us out. Quite the contrary, *submission* enables us to fit in and come along. When we *submit,* we orient ourselves in relation to an already existing authority much like merging onto a freeway. The traffic on the freeway was there before we chose to merge with it. Unless we want to collide, we had better not get into traffic at our own speed. We should match our acceleration to the other cars, so we can slip into a space not presently occupied by another vehicle. The point of *submission* is getting things to fit together harmoniously.

Eve in Relation to Adam

We see this *submission-as-fitting-in* principle in the creative order. God followed a clear sequence in making mankind. He started with Adam—and afterwards made a *"helpmeet"* that was *suitable* for him. None of the animals fit the bill. So, God took Adam's rib and fashioned Eve. She was his counterpart.[67] She *"originated"* from Adam in order to *fit in with* him—in perfect unity. That's what the Bible explains:

[63]Colossians 1:15
[64]Colossians 1:18; Revelation 1:5
[65]Hebrews 1:6
[66]Hebrews 12:23
[67]Genesis 2:18, 22

*"For man does not originate from woman, but woman
from man; for indeed man was not created for the
woman's sake, but woman for the man's sake."*

~ 1 Corinthians 11:8-9

The likelihood of two independently created objects fitting perfectly with one another is rather remote. On the other hand, if one item is made first, it's quite easy to make a counterpart that matches the contours of the first. The English word *woman* is a compound whose root is *man*. Not rocket science, I know, but the simple point radically changes our thoughts about submission: Eve was made in relation to Adam. Adam *"was first created, and then Eve."*[68] He was the first in order, not in rank or superiority. Eve was fully equal with Adam, but Adam was the starting point from which God fashioned his perfect match.

The last part of this passage can easily be misunderstood, too. It sounds like woman was made as a "plaything" for man. *"For man's sake"* is better translated *"through man"* or *"by means of man."* It's the same expression describing how God spoke *"through"* the prophets,[69] or how believers enter into relationship with God *"through"* Christ.[70] You and I are justified *"through"* faith,[71] and all of us exist *"through"* Jesus.[72] Once again, it is a matter of sequence—of one thing leading to or creating another. Because of Jesus, you and I exist. *"He is before all things,"* and, *"all things have been created through Him and for Him."*[73]

> *Another unconscious notion people have is that submission and leadership are mutually exclusive—that they're opposites.*

God did NOT make Eve for the sake (exclusive benefit) of Adam being allowed to use her any way he wanted to use her. She didn't exist to answer his every whim. She wasn't his servant-girl. Rather, in the creative order, Eve was created in relation to him, in *submission* to him—so that she could be *one-with-him*. It is a misreading of Scripture to

---

[68] 1 Timothy 2:13
[69] Matthew 2:23
[70] John 10:9
[71] Romans 3:30
[72] 1 Corinthians 8:6
[73] Colossians 1:16-17

imagine that Eve's submission to Adam somehow signified that she was less than him. God simply wanted to reconnect Eve to Adam after the sad and separate way she had been led into temptation.

Leadership and Submission

Another unconscious notion people have is that submission and leadership are mutually exclusive—that they're opposites. Submitted people must ask permission to do *anything.* Submission means you only listen—and never speak up. Spiritual surrender and submitting to others is for losers. It's for those being led—not for leaders. Leaders don't submit to anyone; that's what makes them leaders! Right? Wrong!

> *Biblically speaking, submission is one of the most powerful aspects of truly spiritual living.*

Godly submission is one of those counter-intuitive, *last-shall-be-first* ways of the Kingdom.[74] Whereas natural, ungodly authority comes from dominating those under us, spiritual authority comes from submitting to those over/before us.[75] Jesus' authority came from His Father, to Whom He submitted.[76] Jesus' leadership flowed from submission—and so does ours. As believers, our only real authority is that which has been given to us by the Lord,[77] and that authority is supposed to be used to build others up, not to put them down.[78]

Biblically speaking, submission is one of the most potent aspects of truly spiritual living. That is why every believer is told to submit to *God,*[79] to *leaders,*[80] to *human authorities,*[81] and to *one another.*[82] Ultimately, submission to others is one of the primary ways we humble ourselves before the *"mighty hand of God,"* and put our trust in Him.[83] Remember what the centurion said to Jesus:

---

[74]See Mark 8:34; Matthew 20:16
[75]See Matthew 20:25-28
[76]Matthew 9:8; 28:18; John 5:27; 17:2
[77]Luke 9:1; 2 Corinthians 10:8
[78]2 Corinthians 10:8; 13:10

[79]James 4:7
[80]Hebrews 13:17
[81]1 Peter 2:13
[82]Ephesians 5:21
[83]1 Peter 5:6-7

"For I also am a man under authority, with soldiers under me; and I say to this one, 'Go!' and he goes, and to another, 'Come!' and he comes, and to my slave, 'Do this!' and he does it."

~ Matthew 8:9

Jesus submitted Himself to God's will by *"taking the form of a bond-servant."*[84] Because of His submitted posture, *"God highly exalted Him"* to the highest position in the cosmos.[85] Christ's attitude is supposed to be our chief aim—*put others first (be sequentially submitted)* and *"regard one another as more important"* than ourselves.[86]

Literally, that means to *place others above* ourselves. In our culture, it sounds marvelously selfless to *place others above* ourselves. It is respectful, voluntary, and other-honoring. But *placing others above* is simply another way of *placing ourselves under (submitting to)* others. Why do we feel noble when we *place others above* ourselves, but somehow foolishly vulnerable when we *place ourselves under* them? In Kingdom culture, the two postures are identical!

> **True authority comes from submission. When we submit to others we trade natural authority for spiritual authority.**

See what happens when we look at true submission outside the context of our limited impressions? We discover that submitting to others is primarily a choice to think more about others than we think about ourselves—*"not merely [to] look out for [our] own personal interests, but also for the interests of others."*[87] In the Kingdom of God, where serving the purposes and people of God is the highest priority, it makes sense, doesn't it, that true authority comes from submission?

In fact, 1 Peter seems to suggest that when we submit to others—even to those who are not living according to God's plan—we trade *natural* authority for *spiritual* authority. Submitting to authorities "over us" doesn't nullify our own authority to lead. Indeed, it is our submission to

---

[84]Philippians 2:7
[85]Philippians 2:6-9

[86]Philippians 2:3
[87]Philippians 2:4

appropriate heads-of-state, heads-of-companies, heads-of-schools, heads-of-homes and heads-of-churches that releases us into the fullest measure of Kingdom authority for our ministry. When leaders cease to be submitted and accountable to others, they become spiritually ineffective and terribly dangerous.

An attitude and lifestyle of submission is appropriate for all believers—especially for spiritual leaders. We do best and experience the most blessing when we arrange ourselves with respect to *all* the God-ordained authorities in our life. Consequently, we are encouraged to *"come under"* or *"fit in with"* a range of authorities. As is the case for men who aspire to leadership, women should submit themselves to mentoring and training, so they become leaders who *"rule well, worthy of double honor,"*[88] as instructed in Scripture.

REVIEW

Before examining the particular Bible passages that have thrown into question the appropriateness of *women-in-ministry-leadership*, I'd like to take a final look at the larger theological and historical picture. In a nutshell, here is the perspective I bring with me as I study the New Testament record:

1. Adam and Eve, as equal expressions of God's creative, like-kind love, were made of the same stuff. They came from one flesh (Adam's). That was God's intentional plan—that they would become and remain one.

2. After their sin, it was necessary for God to adjust His arrangements in order to deal with the drastically changed conditions of His creation. He clothed Adam and Eve to "fix" the nakedness of which they were newly aware.

3. He also sought to mend the breach between man and woman. He did this by requiring something more of each of them in relation to the other.

---

[88] 1 Timothy 5:17

4. In the case of man, God instituted more purposeful *headship*—providing for his wife and her needs (i.e., cultivating crops) by *"giving himself up for her,"* nourishing and cherishing her.[89]

5. Of the woman, God required more purposeful connection to her husband. It was no longer enough that she came from him; she was to be joined with him, as a body to its *head*. Subsequently, he would *"love his own wife as himself."*[90]

6. None of these adjustments by God altered Adam and Eve's co-regency over the earth. As *"head"* and *"body,"* male and female, mankind still had responsibility to act as stewards over the earth.

7. Kingdom ministry, portrayed throughout the Bible, has been carried out by both men and women for millennia. It will continue to do so.

8. Among the potent, spiritual forces that God introduced into the broken cosmos as part of the redemptive order, submission is one of the least understood and appreciated. Submission is not synonymous with complete subjugation or disqualification for ministry.

9. Submission is incumbent upon all believers—not just women. Far from being a disqualifier for ministry leadership, submission at every appropriate level, and to every fitting authority, qualifies believers for greater ministry and leadership.

God is not conflicted. Jesus is the same always.[91] Therefore, it would take an extraordinarily clear statement in the New Testament to move me away from the simple premise that men and women can be used in equal measure to advance the Kingdom of God:

---

[89]Ephesians 5:25–29
[90]Ephesians 5:28, 33
[91]Hebrews 13:8

"...I will pour out My Spirit on all mankind; and your sons and daughters will prophesy..."

~ Joel 2:28

"And I will be a father to you, and you shall be sons and daughters to Me," says the Lord Almighty.

~ 2 Corinthians 6:18

The "Problem" Passages

by Daniel A. Brown, PhD

I do not want to fall into the grievous polarization of opinion that exists in the Church-at-large over the question of *women-in-ministry-leadership*. But I do wish to address several Bible passages that have most often been referenced as reasons why women should be relegated to subservient roles and subjugated positions within Jesus' Church. While I don't insist that everyone accept my viewpoint—as though it is an essential of the faith—I do wish to share my deep convictions about this question.[1]

The Bible is God's inerrant word, and any belief not founded on the truth revealed to us in Scripture will be in error. The view of any church must be drawn from God's written and revealed word. But much of the Church has accepted one *interpretation* of these key passages, the so-called "problem texts," unwittingly presuming that there is no other way to read them in their contextual and cultural setting.

I believe each of these passages can be understood in ways that fit more closely with what the rest of the Bible communicates about the heart of

---

[1]Romans 14:22

God for His children. The brief studies that follow are not meant to be exhaustive—as though I am expounding all the life-material they contain for matters far beyond the particular question we're addressing.

In the interest of keeping this book short and readable, I am aiming my remarks at a popular mind-set within Jesus' Church. It seems like many people pull verses from their context and use short phrases to "prove" what the Bible says about *women-in-ministry-leadership*. I want to pull those quick-quotes back into the whole letters from which they have been lifted.

1 Corinthians 11:1-16

> *"But I want you to understand that Christ is the head of every man, and the man is the head of a woman, and God is the head of Christ. Every man who has something on his head while praying or prophesying disgraces his head. But every woman who has her head uncovered while praying or prophesying disgraces her head, for she is one and the same as the woman whose head is shaved."*

~ 1 Corinthians 11:3-5

The thrust of this passage was to give Corinthian men *and* women detailed instructions for the appropriate way to pray, prophesy and minister publicly in a mixed-gender church setting. Rather than restricting or prohibiting ministry by women, Paul gives *a how-to* lesson to the Corinthian church. Paul's letter describes *women-in-ministry-leadership* as a common occurrence in the early spread of the Gospel.

And yet, these verses are often referenced by people who oppose the concept of women in *public* ministry. They have interpreted Paul's words quite differently than how I read them. Since the very nature of a controversy implies two interpretations of the same thing, I want to acknowledge that this passage is "open to interpretation"—meaning, no one has been able to explain it conclusively.

Some of the Church's inability to arrive at a universal understanding of this text stems from an unusual set of historic facts and a few difficult-to-translate words.

Some of the Church's inability to arrive at a universal understanding of this text stems from an unusual set of historic facts and a few *difficult-to-translate* words. These realities complicate a simple reading of this passage in 21st century English. References to *"the woman whose head is shaved"* make little sense in our day and in our culture, so it is important to put what Paul says in its historic and cultural setting. Let me offer you some pertinent details about the city of Corinth and how those particulars might inform our reading.

Corinth, the City

I have been to Corinth three times, and on each visit, my guides related the same basic facts about the now ruined city. The little reading I have done through the years corroborates their story. Known as the "City of a Thousand (Sacred) Prostitutes," Corinth sat in the shadow of a temple complex high on the mountain ridge that borders the city. That temple was devoted to Aphrodite, the goddess of love. Her priestesses frequented the city (and its baths) in regular processions to and from the temple in plain sight of the populace. This temple, and its peculiar forms of worship, offered visitors and citizens of the city many sanctified temptations.

In addition to its proximity to the temple of love, Corinth was strategically situated at the narrow isthmus separating the Peloponnesian Peninsula from the rest of Greece. Ships putting into port on one side of the isthmus offloaded their crews for the three days it took to drag the boats along a stone causeway, the *dialkos,* and put back to sea on the other side. This overland journey cut more than a week off the sailing time required to circumnavigate the southern landmass and sail north and west toward Rome (Italy). A steady flow of sailors with lengthy shore leave created quite a demand for street and temple prostitutes.

That certainly helped Corinth live up to its reputation as a city of wasted living, debauchery and illicit sex. In fact, a *"Corinthian Girl"* was another name for a prostitute. *"Corithianizing"* was slang for fornicating. In modern language, Corinth was a city where everyone *"did his or her own thing"* without regard for convention or propriety.

In Paul's day, Corinth was a recently-rebuilt, bustling Roman colony. He spent many months in Corinth, so he was familiar with the tug of flesh—and how ruinous it could be to people's walk of faith. His letter to his friends is filled with allusions to Corinth's many temptations. Paul wished that all men were like him—gifted toward a life of unconcerned celibacy, without the temptations that usually afflict men.[1] But, since most men are

---

[1] 1 Corinthians 7:7

not like Paul, he makes several concessions and suggestions for how h. flock in Corinth could decrease temptation.

Illicit sexual activity was so pronounced that Paul suggests believers would be better off if each man had *"his own wife,"* and *"each woman…her own husband."*[2] He has to remind them that *"the body is not for immorality [harlotry], but for the Lord;"*[3] and, *"the one who joins himself to a harlot is one body with her."*[4] Paul offers advice to those resisting temptation, and he makes suggestions to those who are inadvertently tempting their fellow believers.

Paul's Themes

For good Bible study, context is a vital consideration. The historical setting is one kind of context, but not the only kind. What happens or what is said prior to any Bible passage we examine often holds the key for understanding what the passage itself says. I won't bore you with academic details, but words like *juxtaposition, theme* and *context* are huge in the study of literature. All my years at the university ingrained in me the search for larger themes in a book—and how the author returns to those same ideas again and again. First and foremost, a good book communicates a larger message, a theme. The episodes within the whole piece reinforce its basic themes.

Find the theme, and you find the single most important tool for interpreting the storyline and the episodes. The two primary themes I see in Paul's first letter to the Corinthians are:

1. God has equipped every believer to be used in spiritual ministry; and,

2. True spirituality is filled with a love that thinks about and puts others first.

From the first chapter to the last, Paul has a point for writing. He reinforces the message again and again throughout the letter—*"You are*

---

[2]1 Corinthians 7:2   [4]1 Corinthians 6:16
[3]1 Corinthians 6:13

THE "PROBLEM" PASSAGES: 1 CORINTHIANS 11:1-6

y [spiritual] gift,"[5] but "let all that you do be done in love."[6]
he says,"I want you to realize your gifting for ministry, but
_~~ ~u~~ you to be sensitive to those around you when you minister."

Gender or Spouse?—The Language

We will come back to the historic and thematic context for this tricky
passage later, but there is one other internal difficulty, and that is the very
language itself. The language of the day used the same term for *man* as for
husband (anēr), and the same word for *woman* and *wife (gunē).*

Some readers have, thereby, misconstrued Paul's words, *"Christ is the head
of every man/husband, and the man/husband is the head of a woman/wife,"*[7]
to mean that men in general are heads over women. If this is a God-
ordained relationship between the genders, that "order" places all men as
"the head of" all women. It follows, in their view, that no woman can be
"the head of" a man. They also presuppose the meaning of *headship* to be
~~exclusive-rights leadership, and determine that it is always inappropriate for~~
any woman to exercise leadership over (any) man.

However, virtually every student of the Bible agrees that, in an identical
passage found in Ephesians, Paul is not referring to men and women in
general, but to husbands in particular relation to their wives:

> *"For the husband/man is the head of the wife/woman,
> as Christ is the head of the church, He Himself being
> the Savior of the body."*
>
> ~ Ephesians 5:23

Christ is the Bridegroom. God's Spirit jealously desires His Bride to be
His alone.[8] Paul writes the Corinthians another letter in which he says,
"I am jealous for you... for I betrothed you to one husband."[9] Jesus will not
share with others His relationship with His Bride; neither does He want
His beloved ruled over by others. He, and He alone, is the Church's head.

---

[5] 1 Corinthians 1:7
[6] 1 Corinthians 16:14
[7] 1 Corinthians 11:3

[8] James 4:5
[9] 2 Corinthians 11:2

No other has claim to His Bride. In exactly the same way, it is perverse to suggest that all men have an equal claim over one man's wife.

Husbands and wives become one flesh. As one body, they have one head—the husband. But it is overstated to suggest that all men have been joined to all women! While there are other kinds of generalized authority portrayed in Scripture, it is difficult to support the notion of (all) men's *headship* over (all) women.

> *...if we examine the 1 Corinthians text carefully, we see that while it says, "Christ is the head of every man," it does not say "man is the head of every woman."*

Additionally, if we examine the 1 Corinthians text carefully, we see that while it says, *"Christ is the head of every man,"* it does not say, *"man is the head of every woman."* The word "every" is not in the phrase about man and woman. I see no way to interpret Paul's words as a declaration that men, in general, have headship over all women.

SPIRITUAL HEADSHIP

That leads us to an examination of what, exactly, Paul means by *headship.* Does *headship* imply that a wife, whose *head* is her husband, is necessarily restricted from ministry leadership? Does having a *head* in the home (i.e., being someone's wife) preclude having a leadership role in the church? Can a single woman have leadership responsibilities that are denied to a married woman?

> *Headship is only a factor when two have been united into one, and when they are in a covenantal relationship with one another.*

Christ is the *head* of the Church because the Church is His Bride.[10] Headship is only a factor when two have been united into one, and when they are in a covenantal relationship with one another. We are one with Christ,[11] having been joined with Him,[12] so God has given Him as our head:

[10]Revelation 19:7
[11]Romans 12:5; Galatians 3:28
[12]Romans 7:4

39

*"And He put all things in subjection under His feet, and
gave Him as head over all things to the church…"*

~ Ephesians 1:22

We celebrate Christ's headship over the Church and over us because we
understand it as a blessing. In my opinion, the discussion about *women-in-
ministry-leadership* leapfrogs far too quickly to presumptions about what a
word like *headship* means. Many conclusions are based on shaky
definitions.

In English, we often use *"head"* synonymously with "leader" or
"authority" and presume they are somewhat interchangeable. We call the
leaders-of-nations "heads-of-state." In the New Testament, however, the
only comparable expression is used when Jesus refers to the *head-of-the-
household.* [13] It means the head of a family (home)—and doesn't actually
include the Greek word for *head (kephale).*

Head: First Before Others

In the language-of-the-day, *kephale* did not necessarily imply *ruler over,* as
it does in English. Rather, it suggested two slightly different meanings.
One of those concepts could best be translated as *prominence—to be
preeminent, to stand out,* or *to be first in order.* We see this idea in a statement
Paul makes about Jesus:

*"He is also head [kephale]of the body, the church; and
He is the beginning, the firstborn from the dead, so that
He Himself will come to have first place in everything."*

~ Colossians 1:18

> **His headship
> qualifies us for
> ministry; it doesn't
> keep us from it!**

Jesus stands first among us. He has first place
because He leads us into everything God
wants for us. He goes before us as the way-
maker; we follow His lead. He isn't the
winner in a contest against us. He doesn't use

---

[13] Matthew 24:43; Luke 12:39; 13:25

His prominence to prevent us from sharing His authority. Instead, He uses His role as head to reconcile us with God and to give us our full inheritance. His headship qualifies us for ministry; it doesn't keep us from it! Because He is our head, first in order, He declares, *"Follow Me!"*[14]

Jesus brings us into our ministry inheritance because that is what true spiritual *heads* do. If a husband, as head of his wife, follows Jesus' example, that husband will go first in sacrifice, giving himself *"up for her."*[15] He will be the "stand out" example for her to emulate in life and ministry. A head that says to its body, "You may not go where I go," will have a hard time laying claim to leadership (which implies followership), and a hard time getting where it is trying to go. From this definition of *headship,* I see no way to justify keeping women in a limited leadership role.

> *When describing Jesus as Head of the Church, Paul means that Jesus is the source of our spiritual life and growth…*

Head: A Source to Others

The other idea behind the meaning of *kephale* might be translated *source/origin* (as in *beginning* or the *headwaters* of a river). Paul is likely thinking of this meaning when he says, *"For man does not originate from woman, but woman from man."*[16] When describing Jesus as Head of the Church, Paul means that Jesus is the source of our spiritual life and growth (maturity). He is,

> *"…the head, from whom the entire body, being supplied and held together by the joints and ligaments, grows with a growth which is from God."*
>
> ~ Colossians 2:19

He doesn't simply lead the way and leave us to follow as best we can in our own strength. Rather, He provides what we cannot supply. He is, as the old song declares, the "Fount of every blessing." He is the source of

---

[14]Matthew 8:22   [16]1 Corinthians 11:8
[15]Ephesians 5:25

our *"eternal salvation."*[17] That's why Paul has reminded the Corinthians earlier in his letter that whatever gifting or ability they have comes not from themselves, but from Christ.[18]

This concept of *head-as-source* is essential for understanding the parallel statement in reference to the Trinity: *"God is the head of Christ."*[19] Jesus and the Father are One,[20] so it makes little sense to merely speak of Jesus being *ruled over* by the Father. Of course, Jesus was always subject to the Father, who put all things in subjection to Him.[21] There is no question about the Son's submission to the Father's will because He came to the earth exclusively to carry out that will.[22] When He cried out in the Garden, Jesus exclaimed, *"Not My will but Yours be done!"*[23]

But in addition to the obvious authority/submission implications of *headship* that usually enter the debate about the role of *women-in-ministry-leadership*, let's look more closely at this notion of *head-as-source* that we see throughout Jesus' ministry. Perhaps it offers us some new ground for discussion—and amplified roles for both men and women.

Head: A Model for Others

Jesus gave honor to the Father as the source of His teaching and ministry: *"I proceeded forth and have come from God, for I have not even come on My own initiative, but He sent Me."*[24] It wasn't self-initiative or independence that brought Jesus to our world. He did not act of His own accord, under His own volition, or by His own power. He came because He followed His Father—in heart and in action.

Jesus never acted independently of the Father, so what did He do and how did He act? Obviously, Jesus knew what to do and say because He simply followed the Father's example. He did what He observed, and He spoke what He heard—from the One to whom He was submitted:

[17]Hebrews 5:9
[18]1 Corinthians 4:7
[19]1 Corinthians 11: 3
[20]John 10:30
[21]1 Corinthians 15:25, 27-28
[22]Hebrews 10:7
[23]Luke 22:42
[24]John 8:42

"Truly, truly, I say to you, the Son can do nothing of Himself, unless it is something He sees the Father doing; for whatever the Father does, these things the Son also does in like manner. For the Father loves the Son, and shows Him all things that He Himself is doing; and the Father will show Him greater works than these, so that you will marvel."

~ John 5:19-20

This has startling implications for what *headship* means—and for what those under righteous *headship* will end up doing. In complete submission, Jesus followed the words and actions of His Father (Head), who was His model for ministry. Jesus did *"in like manner"* (*homoiōs*) with the Father. The Son copied the Father's words/actions. Similarly, we know Jesus is the Head of the Church, and He tells us that we will do the same things He did—and even greater things![25]

> *Spiritual headship actually promotes people into ministry. It declares, "You can do what I do!"*

Wouldn't that suggest that a woman, in complete submission to her husband (head), will be released to do *"in like manner"* any ministry her husband does? Our English language has betrayed us into thinking that submission (to an authority) disallows full partnership and participation. What we see in the headship and submission modeled by the Father and Son is exactly opposite to that notion. *Spiritual headship actually promotes people into ministry. It declares, "You can do what I do!"* God sent Jesus into the world to minister and teach. Why would earthly *"heads"* presume to do differently?

STUMBLING BLOCKS

The Corinthian Christians apparently needed some practical lessons for how to avoid *"offending"* others or placing a *"stumbling block"* in their path. The new-found giftings, revelations, life-patterns and freedoms these new Christians were experiencing left them vulnerable to excess and insensitivity. Throughout the letter, Paul celebrates the richness of the

---

[25]John 14:12

Corinthians' spiritual inheritance, but he also cautions them to be sensitive to those around them. Consequently, he points out inadvertent ways in which they created difficulties for others.

Divisions, quarrels and factions built around human personalities demonstrated just how *"fleshly"* they were.[26] Immoralities that would have made even the Corinthians blush, were being tolerated in the church.[27] Believers were in legal proceedings against believers;[28] some Christians were still visiting prostitutes;[29] meat-eaters were boasting of their freedom to eat;[30] some people were treating the Lord's Supper as little more than a potluck;[31] church services sometimes slid off into chaotic and random displays of spiritual gifts;[32] etc.

Because Paul did not want his friends to be unaware of their gifts,[33] much of his letter offers instruction for how to function in those gifts. He explains what they are—and how they work best. But, as I've mentioned before, he also wanted his friends to realize that they should exercise restraint in their new-found Christian life:

> **The whole point of ministry is serving others.**

"All things are lawful, but not all things edify. Let no one seek his own [good], but that of his neighbor."[34] They should think of others. That's what love does.[35]

A key aspect of true spirituality is the determination to "please others," rather than ourselves. The whole point of ministry is serving others. *"Take care,"* Paul cautions, *"that this liberty of yours does not somehow become a stumbling block to the weak."[36]* In the verses just prior to the passage we are examining (i.e., the immediate context), Paul reiterates his main theme. He cautions the Corinthians not to eat meat they knew had been offered to idols (because it could violate another's conscience):

---

[26]1 Corinthians 3:1-9

[27]1 Corinthians 5:1-13

[28]1 Corinthians 6:1-8

[29]1 Corinthians 6:12-20

[30]1 Corinthians 8:1-13

[31]1 Corinthians 11:23-34

[32]1 Corinthians 12-14

[33]1 Corinthians 12:1

[34]1 Corinthians 10:23-24

[35]1 Corinthians 13:1-13

[36]1 Corinthians 8:9

*"...whatever you do, do all to the glory of God. Give no
offense either to Jews or to Greeks or to the church of
God; just as I also please all men in all things, not
seeking my own profit but the profit of the many, so that
they may be saved."*

~ 1 Corinthians 10:31-33

What's the Big Deal?

He reminds them not to let their newfound freedoms in dress and church
ministry cause anyone to stumble. If anything we do creates difficulty or
temptation for fellow Christians, that is reason enough for us to foreswear
it.[37] Why might Paul preface his discussion about *spiritual headship*—and
head coverings—with this reminder not to *"give offense"* or *"stumble"*
fellow believers? What might have offended the Greeks or Jews in Corinth?
What was the big deal about short hair and head coverings in Paul's day?

The answer brings us back to the historical and geographic context of
this letter. It is my understanding that *Corinthian girls* who worked as
acolytes in the temple of love could be distinguished from average citizens
by means of their very short haircuts. A short-haired woman not wearing
a head-covering or wrap was announcing her connection with the
goddess of love, as well as her availability for "consultation."

No wonder, then, the public display of uncovered female heads in church
services caused unnecessary temptation and speculation among the
newly-converted men. A woman without a covering (either long hair or
a head-scarf) would have been, in effect, stimulating men to remember
their former lifestyle.

Additionally, a married woman who removed her head-covering while
ministering in Jesus' Name would be sending a strong—and confusing—
message to her church family. She would be interpreted as declaring,
*"I am independent of my husband, and I am acting of my own volition, without
any reflection of or connection to him."*

---

[37] 1 Corinthians 8:13

In Corinth Paul contextualizes his suggestion for married *women-in-ministry-leadership* to have their heads covered. He wants them to understand the principle of submission for their own sakes personally—that they are connected in God's redemptive scheme of things in a family that originates with God himself. He also wants them to communicate that truth to others—especially newer believers. Wearing a head covering or having long hair made two simultaneous statements:

1. "I am a daughter of the King, and my life-service has been paid for by my Redeemer. I belong to Him and my husband. I am not for hire by a goddess or by any man."

2. I am submitted to and connected with my spiritual family, in proper order. I am joined together with my husband, as he is joined to me, and we are joined to Christ.

This brief explanation does not deal with all the complexities of the passage, but one final comment may be helpful. Paul allows for the fact that all cultures do not have the same perspective on head-coverings and short hair for women when he says, *"Judge for yourselves..."*[38] The cultural symbols from that day that signified a woman's alignment and connection with appropriate authority in her life are not the critical issue for Paul. What is important to him is that a woman acknowledges such a *fitting* in her life.

> *Women who live in appropriate submission to the authorities in their lives are fully capable and completely authorized to prophesy to men— as well as to women.*

Everyone who seeks to minister in the church ought to be *covered by* and *submitted to* others. That does not mean, however, that women are disallowed from public ministry and leadership. From this text, I have a simple "take-away." Women who live in appropriate *submission* to the authorities in their lives are fully capable and completely authorized to prophesy and minister to men— as well as to women.

---

[38] 1 Corinthians 11:13

1 Corinthians 14:26-40

*"The women are to keep silent in the churches; for they are
not permitted to speak, but are to subject [submit]
themselves, just as the Law also says. If they desire to
learn anything, let them ask their own husbands at home;
for it is improper for a woman to speak in church."*

~ 1 Corinthians 12:34-35

How can one argue with such a straightforward statement, *"The women
are to keep silent in the churches"?* Taken out of context from the entire
letter and from the totality of Scripture, the declaration seems quite
conclusive. However, as we have just read in the same letter, Paul
previously spoke about the appropriate way for a woman to speak a
prophecy aloud in church.[1] Therefore, this admonishment, coming three
chapters later, cannot reasonably be interpreted to prohibit women from
all manner of public speech in church. Women undoubtedly ministered
in the church at Corinth.

That's what I mean by context. What has been said before often
modifies what we think is being said later. What is that message in this
part of his letter? *"Learn how to use your gifting and freedom in Christ for
the sake of others."*

Paul's focus deals with public assemblies of believers, like church
gatherings. Paul reminds believers that everything done and said in
church should *"be done for [the] edification"* of all those gathered, and not
just for the benefit and instruction of a few individuals.[2] Prophecy that
speaks to the whole congregation is far preferable to a prayer in tongues
that speaks to God (and, therefore, ignores those sitting nearby).[3] A church
service is quite different from a prayer closet.

Paul says that, in a public setting, *"five words"* that instruct, strengthen,
encourage or console everyone present are more spiritual than *"ten*

---

[1] 1 Corinthians 11:5
[2] 1 Corinthians 14:26
[3] 1 Corinthians 14:3-5

thousand" unclear, incomprehensible or irrelevant words prayed in a heavenly language.[4] Personal edification is a fabulous goal in the prayer closet, but private devotional patterns must be modified when we are in public. Otherwise, chaos ensues. That is why, during a gathering of believers, a prophecy is more fitting than a message in tongues, unless there is an interpretation of the tongue.[5]

Paul's correction of the Corinthian believers has not been limited to vocal outbursts. Remember, he has also corrected their self-centered identification as members of factions within the church and their disregard for how meat-eating affects others. Even how some of them approached the Lord's Supper—taking too much bread or wine—had affected others negatively.

Some Corinthians have even become so self-absorbed that they believe they are self-sufficient and have no need of any other member of the Body. There is a purpose as to how God has arranged everything for His Church:

> *"...there may be no division in the body, but that the*
> *members may have the same care for one another."*
>
> ~ 1 Corinthians 12:25

Paul admonishes them to care for and about others. The message comes through again and again throughout Paul's letter. When we take that angle of focus on what he says to the women about remaining silent, we discover a few often overlooked details.

"Keep Silent" #1

Let's begin with the phrase itself. Paul uses the expression, *"keep silent [in church],"* three different times in this chapter. Each time he addresses a different category of people attending services. In the first instance, he aims his correction at people who speak or pray in tongues when no interpreter is present: *"Let him [the one who would speak in tongues] keep*

---

[4] 1 Corinthians 14:19   [5] 1 Corinthians 14:13

silent in the church."[6] A public service is not the place or the time for *devotional-closet-liberties* like conversations with God in tongues.[7]

When we are alone in God's presence, there is very little chance of misunderstanding. No one is bothered or confused by what we do in our private times with Jesus. In a group of people, however, we're supposed to think about others and avoid doing anything that might make them stumble over truth. In a public assembly, newcomers will conclude that Christians are mad barbarians if the members of the assembly speak aloud in tongues without interpretation.[8]

Plus, fellow believers will receive no benefit from what is spoken. They cannot understand what is being said, so they have no way to appropriate the truth for themselves. You can hear the echo of Paul's previous words:

> *"If I speak with the tongues of men and of angels, but*
> *do not have love, I have become a noisy gong or a*
> *clanging cymbal."*

> ~ 1 Corinthians 13:1

Noisy gongs should hold their tongues. Of course, Paul wants all his friends to speak in tongues, but not in church—at least, not without an interpretation: *"If there is no interpreter, let him keep silent in church; and let him speak to himself and to God."*[9] In other words, instead of speaking loudly enough to be heard throughout the room, *speakers-in-tongues* should keep their prayers in their minds or as mere whispers on their lips.

But this text does not, in any way, imply that those who speak aloud in tongues without an interpretation were being banned from ministry leadership in church for the rest of their lives. They were simply being encouraged to tone down their spiritual excitement.

> *People receive more benefit in an assembly if everything is "done properly and in an orderly manner."*

---

[6] 1 Corinthians 14:28
[7] 1 Corinthians 14:2
[8] 1 Corinthians 14:11, 23
[9] 1 Corinthians 14:28

"Keep Silent" #2

"God is not a God of confusion," Paul writes.[10] People receive more benefit in an assembly if everything is *"done properly and in an orderly manner."*[11] That's why Paul instructs, *"prophesy one by one,"* instead of allowing everyone to prophesy simultaneously.[12] He suggests that they cluster two or three revelations together, and evaluate them before moving on to the next set.[13] Should the Spirit give a revelation to someone while another person is speaking, Paul says (for the second time in this chapter), *"Let him [the one who is currently speaking] keep silent."*[14]

Prophecy is precisely the gift that Paul most encourages the Corinthians to pursue. It is appropriate in church because it edifies, exhorts and consoles all those present. A prophecy might reveal the secrets of someone's heart—thereby bringing them to salvation. A prophecy might assure fellow believers that God knows their exact situation—and assure them that He is in control. In whatever manner a prophetic word comes forth in a public assembly, it builds people up.

Not a single negative tone attaches itself to Paul's view of prophecy. He is not against prophets or prophecy. And yet, he makes clear that there are times for *prophecy-givers* to keep silent. When it is another's turn to prophesy, the one whose turn it was previously should stop talking. Can you hear the reference to *order* and *sequential submission?* Some otherwise legitimate spiritual activity is inappropriate in certain settings or at certain times. If it is out of order, it is not placing others above itself.

It's as though Paul is saying, "When it's no longer your place to speak, keep quiet so others can continue the ministry to the whole assembly." Because so many individuals in the early church came to the meetings prepared to minister—quite a different scenario from today's arrangements wherein people come expecting to receive ministry—each one needed a turn:

---

[10] 1 Corinthians 14:33
[11] 1 Corinthians 14:40
[12] 1 Corinthians 14:31

[13] 1 Corinthians 14:29
[14] 1 Corinthians 14:30

"What is the outcome then, brethren? When you assemble, each one has a psalm, has a teaching, has a revelation, has a tongue, has an interpretation. Let all things be done for edification. But if a revelation is made to another who is seated, the first one must keep silent. For you can all prophesy one by one, so that all may learn and all may be exhorted…"

~ 1 Corinthians 14:26, 30-31

Perpetual talkers, even prophetic ones, should *"keep quiet"* when their talking is out of order. When prophets who have been expounding some revelation from God are instructed to yield the pulpit and *"keep silent,"* Paul certainly is not intending to exclude such

> *Perpetual talkers, even prophetic ones, should "keep quiet" when their talking is out of order.*

ministers from future public ministry! Rather, he wants to move them from self-absorption to self-control.

The spirits of Christian prophets remain *"subject"* to them.[15] In other words, prophets can, and should, control themselves. They should not blurt out prophecy in catatonic, trance-like utterances, similar to the supposed prophecies of the Sibyl or Oracle of Delphi, whose utterances were induced by hallucinogenic vapors.[16] Disorderly outbursts by people who lose control of their faculties are out of sync with a God who arranges things in an *"orderly manner."* The Greek word used here *(taxi)* means *"an arrangement with a fixed succession."*

> *When read in the context of the whole letter…it's clear that Paul cannot be speaking to all women for all time.*

"Keep Silent" #3

After first admonishing disorderly *speakers-in-tongues* and *stop-not-prophets* who refused to be quiet when it was another's turn, Paul directs his

---

[15] The Sibyl was the female medium who prophesied and predicted the future. The temple complex at Delphi was located roughly 50 miles north of Corinth across the Corinthian Gulf, and its cult following was prevalent throughout the Mediterranean world.

[16] 1 Corinthians 14:34

corrective comments to a third category of people: *"Let the women keep silent in the churches."*[17] When read in the context of the whole letter, especially his instructions for how women ought to prophesy in church, it's clear that Paul cannot be speaking to all women for all time.

He is addressing particular groups of women who—like *stop-not-prophets* and *speakers-in-tongues*—were adding confusion in church assemblies. They were not controlling their urge to speak aloud, and that put them out of sync with the group setting. They were literally *"out of order."*

Paul goes on to say that such disorderly women should *"subject themselves."*[18] There is that *submission* word again *(hupotassō)*. In subjecting myself, I orient myself in relation to an already existing authority. The point of submission is getting things to fit together harmoniously. The women are being told, in no uncertain terms, to control themselves and recognize they are distracting the whole assembly.

Paul's use of the word *"subject,"* when lifted out of context, is the basis upon which some church traditions equate women's submission with their silence in church. Such groups believe that a truly submitted woman will not engage in public, spoken ministry or ministry that benefits/affects men.

But the call for talkative women to *"subject"* themselves is simply an echo of the admonition Paul has already given to *stop-not-prophets* and public *speakers-in-tongues.* All three groups of people should control themselves, think about others, and behave appropriately. They ought not seek their own or *"act unbecomingly."*[19] Their exuberance over a newly experienced spiritual facility caused them to be insensitive to the public setting and to others around them.

LIFETIME BAN?

Paul admonishes these groups; he does not banish them from ministry. Women were, for the first time in their lives, receiving structured spiritual instruction. Having been denied the sort of religious training afforded to

---

[17]1 Corinthians 14:34   [18]1 Corinthians 13:5   [19]1 Corinthians 13:5

men, they would have had many questions—and a great deal of excitement about what was being taught. Women talking out of turn and loudly enough to distract the proceedings of a service, even if it was to ask their husbands something because they wanted to learn, would be behaving *"improperly."*

Still in the habit of much less formal and far more individualized instruction at home or with a few close girl-friends, the *talking-women* made the same blunder in public as the *speakers-in-tongues*. Small-group family settings are completely different from large-group public ones. Just as some things are perfectly acceptable in the prayer closet, but not in church, so some habits and behaviors from the home-study setting do not transfer well into the public arena.

> **Both men and women were present at those meetings, so we must assume both men and women exercised their gifts, including teaching, singing, prophesying, etc.**

I do not see any reason to interpret Paul's statements about *talking-women* who were disrupting the service as a general restriction on *women-in-ministry-leadership*. If I chose that interpretation, I would need to apply it in a parallel fashion to the other two groups he mentions. If it is nonsensical to restrict the future ministry assignments of *stop-not-prophets* and anyone who has ever *spoken-aloud-in-tongues* without an interpreter, it is also nonsensical to disallow *women-in-ministry-leadership*.

By the way, why do most readers assume the *stop-not-prophets* and *speakers-in-tongues* were only men? Paul has already explained the proper way for women to exercise the gift of prophecy in church; consequently, we know he permitted and encouraged women to prophesy. Furthermore, he says, *"You may all prophesy,"*[20] and *"when you assemble, each one has a psalm, has a teaching..."*[21] Both men *and* women were present at those meetings, so we must assume both men *and* women exercised their gifts, including teaching, singing, prophesying, etc.

---

[20]1 Corinthians 14:31   [21]1 Corinthians 14:26

Ephesians 5:21-6:9

> *"... and be subject to one another in the fear of Christ.*
> *Wives, be subject to your own husbands, as to the Lord.*
> *For the husband is the head of the wife, as Christ also*
> *is the head of the church, He Himself being the Savior*
> *of the body. But as the church is subject to Christ, so*
> *also the wives ought to be to their husbands in*
> *everything."*
>
> ~ Ephesians 5:21-24

When we extract a Bible verse and read it without the benefit of its surrounding context, we often arrive at an interpretation quite different

> *Submission is not as one-dimensional as some people seem to think. And it certainly isn't just women who are instructed to submit in life.*

from what the writer intended. One of the most common and glaring instances of this is when people quote what becomes a soundbite: *"Wives be subject to your own husbands as to the Lord."*[1]

Contrary to popular belief, this passage in Ephesians is not primarily about husbands and wives—or some uniquely restrictive *submission* incumbent upon married women—but about what every believer, male and female and young and old, ought to do to *fit in with* the rest of the Body. *Submission* is not as one-dimensional as some people seem to think. And it certainly isn't just women who are instructed to *submit* in life.

The issue of *women-in-ministry-leadership* should not be confused with *women-in-marriage,* but sincere believers sometimes blur them together—especially in this passage. Much, though not all, of the confusion about the appropriateness of women providing spiritual leadership to men is due to this type of contextual error.

We have already studied how God arranged redemptive patterns in the broken cosmos. One of those patterns is the power of *joint-surrender.*

---

[1]Ephesians 5:22

Unity comes through mutual *submission—putting others above ourselves.* The pattern works in marriage—*and* it works in church. A couple will flourish by being *"subject to one another."²* So will Christ's body experience amazing bounty when believers *place others above* themselves.

> **Unity comes through mutual submission— putting others above ourselves.**

There are many different situations and mixes of people who live in various degrees of submission with one another. Peter tells us all, *"for the Lord's sake...,"³* to find appropriate points of submission within our life-setting. He presents us with a comprehensive litany of people-groups who can and should fit in with others: *"servants...to masters";⁴ "wives...to husbands";⁵ "husbands...with wives";⁶ "younger men...to elders"* and *"all of you...toward one another."⁷*

Likewise, Paul addresses several categories of people in this letter, and admonishes each of them to be *"subject to one another in the fear of Christ."⁸* That statement is the launch point for the entire passage. In the verses that follow, Paul gives *husbands, wives, children, fathers, slaves* and *masters* similar counsel for spiritual living.

> **Societal and class distinctions between people in the secular culture of that day disappeared in the congregational gatherings of individuals who were newly adopted by God.**

Counter-Culture

There was a simple reason for Paul to address each of these diverse categories of society. Societal and class distinctions between people in the secular culture of that day disappeared in the congregational gatherings of individuals who were newly adopted by God.⁹ *Slaves* sang hymns or joined hands in prayer with their *masters;* teenagers who had accepted Christ months earlier watched their *fathers* get baptized; *husbands* and

---

²Ephesians 5:21
³1 Peter 2:13-16
⁴1 Peter 2:18
⁵1 Peter 3:1
⁶1 Peter 3:7
⁷1 Peter 5:5
⁸Ephesians 5:21
⁹Ephesians 1:5

wives, who were once dead in their trespasses and sins,[10] found themselves as joint-heirs in Christ.

How should fellow-Christians behave toward one another? How easy it would have been for a *slave* to use her newfound freedom in Christ as an opportunity to disrespect her *mistress,* now also a believer and attending the same cell group. As a Spirit-filled believer, the young slave-girl might speak to her mistress *"in psalms and hymns and spiritual songs,"*[11] during the course of the house-group meeting. What should she do the following day when her status reverts to that of a household slave?

Paul encourages each segment of the church to be *"devoted to one another in brotherly love"* and to honor one another above themselves.[12] Rather than using their spiritual freedom to throw off appropriate respect in the home, they were to redouble their determination to defer to one another. They were to place others above themselves. There is a lesson for us today.

Submission and Authority

Appropriate submission in one arena of life does not disqualify believers for leadership in other areas. Each life-situation has ways in which we can honor the Lord by honoring *(submitting to* and *giving greater regard to)* others. No more submission is being required of one group than of another because *"there is no partiality"* in Christ.[13]

Would we propose that submission, by a man, to civic authorities disqualifies him from sharing God's Word with those authorities if the opportunity presented itself? Of course not. A man who submits to his company's CEO can still teach an adult Sunday school class that might include that CEO as a member.

Likewise, though called to submit to spiritual leaders in his church,[14] a man does not surrender his leadership role within his family. If he serves his wife, he is not excluded from ministry service outside the home; on

---

[10]Ephesians 2:1   [12]Romans 12:10   [14]Hebrews 13:17
[11]Ephesians 5:19   [13]Ephesians 6:9

the contrary, his spiritual activity will be *"hindered"* if he does not esteem her as a *fellow heir.*[15] Why, then, should a wife be excluded from spiritual leadership outside the home simply because she submits to her own husband and trusts in the Lord?[16]

We can put Paul's words in present-day language and follow the logic of his argument: he tells employees to obey and be subject to their employers *"with fear and trembling...as to Christ."*[17] But he doesn't mean that all employed believers (submitted to their own employers at their places of work) should obey all the believers who are employers. Nor does it suggest that *submitted-to-a-boss* employees are disqualified from leadership in the Church.

> *Being subject to one's husband "as to the Lord," does not mean that a married woman is supposed to orient herself with respect to other women's husbands in church.*

In exactly the same way, we cannot, from this text, imply that a married woman should *come under* and *fit in with* all husbands—or to men in general. *Being subject* to one's husband *"as to the Lord,"* does not mean that a married woman is supposed to orient herself with respect to other women's husbands in church. Neither does *being subject* to one's employer *"as to Christ,"* mean that all employees in any company should submit themselves to all church-going executives.

The Church puts no restrictions on leadership roles that can be filled by members engaged in the marketplace or submitted to a boss. It is a mystery why some church traditions disqualify other church members from similar leadership roles *just because* they are submitted to a husband. Granted, husbands and bosses are not synonymous. The point is that every believer has people to whom they submit. Submission is an all-inclusive assignment for us all, so why do some people single out one particular point of submission and use it as a disqualifier for *ministry-leadership?*

---

[15]1 Peter 3:7

[16]1 Peter 3:1

[17]Ephesians 6:5

Heavenly Giftings

It should be noted, as well, that Paul continues his letter with one of the most significant passages in the New Testament concerning the nature of our spiritual battle on earth. He encourages all believers—men and women, slaves and masters, children and parents—to *"be strong in the Lord…take up the full armor of God…and stand firm [against]* *"spiritual forces of wickedness in the heavenly places."*[18] This echoes the beginning of Ephesians when he makes an incredible assertion to all believers—without mention of gender, marital status or position in society—that we have been blessed with *"every spiritual blessing in the heavenly places in Christ…"*[19]

> **The only ministry distinctions Paul mentions in his letter are based on gifting, not gender,…**

This grand perspective positions *every* son *and* daughter of God in the heavenlies as examples of His grace,[20] and on earth as agents of that grace. If women are not excluded or limited in those arrangements, why would the Church impose restrictions on which church-related roles can be filled by them? The only ministry distinctions Paul mentions in his letter are based on gifting, not gender, and their primary function is for *"equipping the saints for the work of service."*[21]

There is no mention of gender in the Ministry Gift-Mixes (apostle, prophet, evangelist, etc.), and certainly no suggestion that believers are equipped differently based on their life-situations—married, slave, etc. Instead, Paul affirms the value of everyone working together as equals in love, *"according to the proper working of each individual part."*[22] No basis can be found in this text for any limitations on the nature or degree of ministry available for women.

> **It seems far more congruent with God's plan to view men and women as joint-heirs with Christ, even as Gentiles (not just Jews) are "fellow heirs and fellow members of the body."**

---

[18]Ephesians 6:10-18 [20]Ephesians 2:6-7 [22]Ephesians 4:16
[19]Ephesians 1:3 [21]Ephesians 4:12

Because some issues are not categorically spelled out and precisely defined in the Bible, it's important to give grace to other people and their perspectives. But it is difficult to see how gender can be made into a category of gifting or be a basis for exclusion from certain parts of Christ's Body. It seems far more congruent with God's plan to view men and women as joint-heirs with Christ, even as Gentiles (not just Jews) are *"fellow heirs and fellow members of the body."*[23]

---

[23]Ephesians 3:6

1 Timothy 2:8-15

"Therefore I want the men in every place to pray, lifting up holy hands, without wrath and dissension. Likewise, I want women to adorn themselves with proper clothing, modestly and discreetly, not with braided hair and gold or pearls or costly garments, but rather by means of good works, as is proper for women making a claim to godliness."

~ 1 Timothy 2:8-10

"A woman must quietly receive instruction with entire submissiveness. But I do not allow a woman to teach or exercise authority over a man, but to remain quiet. For it was Adam who was first created, and then Eve. And it was not Adam who was deceived, but the woman being deceived, fell into transgression."

~ 1 Timothy 2:11-14

Once again, to truly understand the meaning of this passage, we must understand the purpose for Paul's letters. Timothy's first pastorate was located in Ephesus, one of the largest cities in the Roman Empire at that time. At the crossroads of the great caravan route stretching east toward India and the shipping lanes that brought goods from all over the Mediterranean, Ephesus was one of the wildest and most idolatrous cities in the Empire. Paul discipled a small band of believers there. As a result of his teaching (over a couple of years), the whole region heard the gospel. The Church radically affected the culture—so much so, that the pagan society rose up against the Church.[1]

With little formal preparation, Timothy was appointed as lead pastor of the sizeable congregation in Ephesus. Sometime later, Paul writes two letters (1 & 2 Timothy) with advice and counsel for leading the congregation Paul knew so well. Timothy was under personal attack, probably based on his age and inexperience.[2] Furthermore, because he

---

[1] Acts 19 [2] 1 Timothy 4:12; 5:1

was correcting several false teachers and leaders who had a foothold in the church,[3] those leaders were undoubtedly resisting the young pastor.

False doctrines and misleading spiritual values permeated the church, so Paul's foremost advice to Timothy was to replace wrong-spirited leaders with truly godly ones. Reminding Timothy of the primacy of love as the goal for all teaching,[4] Paul paints portraits of five different types of pseudo-spiritual leaders, and contrasts the qualities of those problematic people with characteristics that ought to be true of leaders in the church. His advice in the first two chapters follows a basic pattern: *"Instead of quality X, look for quality Y in those who want to be leaders."*

Pseudo-Leaders

Specifically, Paul counsels Timothy not to fill his leadership ranks with seemingly notable people like:

1. *Mystics* who *speculate* about matters God has not revealed in His word, rather than *believe* what He has said;[5]

2. *Legalists* who lose sight of grace, and try to bring others into condemnation;[6]

3. *Former leaders* who have suffered spiritual shipwreck, and no longer live as they once did;[7]

4. *Attention-grabbing* men who imagine that blustering opinions and debate accomplish more than prayer;[8] and,

5. *Eye-catching women* who adorn themselves with high fashion, instead of with good works.[9]

When Paul says, *"I want men...to pray...without wrath or dissension,"*[10] he draws a distinction for Pastor Timothy between readily apparent, outward

---

[3] 1 Timothy 1:3-4
[4] 1 Timothy 1:5
[5] 1 Timothy 1:3-4
[6] 1 Timothy 1:7-16
[7] 1 Timothy 1:19-20
[8] 1 Timothy 2:8
[9] 1 Timothy 2:9
[10] 1 Timothy 2:8

> *A woman can demonstrate her maturity "by means of good works," serving without being disquieted herself, or disquieting others.*

qualities and those truer manifestations of godliness behind the scenes. It is possible for men to appear spiritual simply by virtue of being opinionated or passionate about things. But Paul wants to know, *"Can they pray?"*

A man who might be able to intimidate leaders or impose his will on fellow believers with a loud or threatening demeanor, will not, with those same tools, be able to accomplish the will of God.[11] Debate and opinion will not push back spiritually malignant forces. Only prayer makes the gospel-kind of difference. Paul wants praying leaders serving in church as good examples to others.

"Likewise," he advises Timothy to choose leaders who do not confuse physical attractiveness with spiritual beauty.[12] A man's spiritual depth cannot be measured by an opinion statement, a shaken fist or a raised voice; neither is a woman's *"claim to godliness"* to be found in a fashion statement, expensive outfits or jewel-accented hairstyles.[13] Prayer *"without wrath or dissension"* backs up a man's claim to spiritual maturity.[14] A woman can demonstrate her maturity *"by means of good works,"* serving without being disquieted herself, or disquieting others.[15]

Godly Leaders

Paul recommends that Timothy choose leaders who know when and how to submit. Instead of debating and rising up in public indignation, *men-in-ministry-leadership* should model a peaceable demeanor. They ought to recognize spiritual authorities in the church. So should *women-in-ministry-leadership.* When they *"receive instruction"* or correction, Paul notes, they should embrace it *"quietly...with entire submissiveness."*[16] Can they resist the temptation to rise up in self-importance to intimidate the very leaders who have corrected them? In effect, Paul poses simple

[11]James 1:20
[12]1 Timothy 2:9
[13]1 Timothy 2:9
[14]1 Timothy 2:8
[15]1 Timothy 2:10
[16]1 Timothy 2:11

questions about anyone Timothy might consider for leadership in his church:

1. *Can a man keep his opinions to himself and pray about the matters he feels so strongly, or does he tend to raise his voice above all others in an effort to get his way?*

2. *Can a woman hold her tongue and keep her seat when she is being corrected, or does she try to dominate the leaders with an "I-know-better" attitude?*

UNSUITABLE AUTHORITY

Paul tells Timothy, *"I do not allow a woman to teach or exercise authority over a man..."*[17] Because the English language lacks the many specific words that the Greek language employs to convey various types of *authority,* our generic understanding of authority in English creates confusion about the permissibility of a woman having authority in a church. The expression translated *"exercise authority over" (authentein)* describes someone who acts with self-appointed authority to seize control of a situation or organization. In this verse, Paul uses a word for authority that is used nowhere else in Scripture.

He does not use the word *(exousia),* the rank held by a military officer positioned above others,[18] or the *capacity* with which Jesus taught, forgave sins, did all that He did—and passed along to His disciples.[19] Among the other words for authority that Paul chose not to use is the *competency* given to spiritual leaders *"for building up"* the saints,[20] or *"rulers [huperoche] who are in authority."*[21] He does not refer to the *weight (baros)* he could exert as an apostle,[22] or the *command (epitage)* with which Titus was told to *"speak and exhort and reprove."*[23] Nor does Paul employ the words for *positional lordship (kuriotes)* or for exercising *control over (exousiazo)* one's own body or will.[24]

---

[17]1 Timothy 2:12
[18]Matthew 8:9
[19]Matthew 7:29; 9:6; 21:27; 28:18-19
[20]2 Corinthians 10:8; 13:10

[21]1 Timothy 2:2
[22]1 Thessalonians 2:6
[23]Titus 2:15
[24]1 Corinthians 7:4

> *Eve's fatal error was to act on her own, subject to nothing except her own judgment, her own consideration and her own wishes...*

He's talking very specifically about women who cannot receive vicarious instruction from those who know more. Such disregard for authority is exactly what caused Eve to take the fruit. Before Eve had been formed from Adam's rib, God gave Adam instruction not to eat of *"the tree of the knowledge of good and evil."*[25] Adam later instructed Eve and told her of God's command. That's why she was able to repeat God's words to the Serpent—she learned them from Adam.[26]

Near the end of this passage, Paul references Eve as the one who *"fell into transgression."* His point is that she disregarded Adam's instruction. She was not alive when God commanded Adam about the tree, so she did not receive God's command herself. Because she regarded her first-hand reasoning above second-hand teaching, she took and ate. Eve's fatal error was to act on her own, subject to nothing except her own judgment, her own consideration and her own wishes—all of which were manipulated by the Serpent.

> *...Paul tells Timothy to disqualify (for ministry leadership) all those who cannot govern their lives by what they learn from others.*

Leaders who are a law unto themselves—who regard their own perspective above that of their mentors and teachers—are dangerous. In effect, Paul tells Timothy to disqualify (for ministry leadership) all those who cannot govern their lives by what they learn from others. *"It was Adam who was first created, and then Eve."*[27] Of necessity, then, Eve had to make a choice—would she live according to what a teacher (Adam) taught her about God's word, or would she question its validity and applicability for herself?

The Serpent offered Eve an alternative teaching. Adam told her God said one thing; the devil told her another.[28] There is the trap. If an aspiring

[25]Genesis 2:17
[26]Genesis 2:16-17
[27]Genesis 2:18, 22; 1 Timothy 2:13
[28]Genesis 3:1, 4-5

leader tries to turn the situation upside down when being corrected, it is a tell-tale sign of danger ahead. When a woman is corrected by a leader's teaching, Paul wants Timothy to watch if she will accept it, or refute it. Does she put her thoughts and conclusions first, and others' teaching second? If so, watch out! In other words, Paul is saying, *"I do not allow a woman [who has just been instructed] to teach or exercise authority over a man."*[29]

Choose leaders carefully. What looks spiritual and impressive isn't always.

Once we realize that Paul is speaking against women presuming to take charge by means of self-appointed authority, the text reads quite differently: beware of women who, after being corrected, rise up over the one correcting them in a challenging and confrontational manner. Such women who *"usurp authority"* are unsuitable for spiritual leadership. They manifest the opposite of what ought to be true of godly leaders—selfless surrender, sacrifice and submission.[30]

PEACEABLE DEMEANOR

To me, it's clear that Paul's warning doesn't apply only to women, unless we also want to suggest that Paul's desire for prayer and lifted hands among male leaders applies only to men. Potential spiritual leaders, both men and women,[31] should not be *"quarrelsome,"*[32] *"self-willed, quick-tempered, pugnacious, but self-controlled."*[33] Paul sought leaders with a peaceable demeanor, as opposed to a contrary, insubordinate one.

> *This attitude of submission is the baseline for simple, godly living and has nothing specifically to do with gender.*

This attitude of submission is the baseline for simple, godly living and has nothing specifically to do with gender. Even believers who do not aspire to leadership ought to behave in a mutually submitted posture of graciousness, obedience and servant-heartedness. An admonition to all

---

[29]1 Timothy 2:12
[30]Romans 12:10; Philippians 2:2-8
[31]2 Timothy 2:8, 10-11
[32]2 Timothy 2:24
[33]Titus 1:7-9

believers should not be used to single out any one group of believers—
as though the call to be submitted is, somehow, more applicable to
women than to men.

This phrase, so frequently used to deny women positions of spiritual
authority, was simply intended to address one type of illegitimate and ill-
gotten authority: authority that has been wrested from the hands of
rightful leaders; authority that relies more on inner reasonings or mystical
knowledge; authority that forces everyone to fit in with and come under
it. Spiritual wisdom—for men *and* women—manifests itself through
"deeds in the gentleness of wisdom,"[34] not in self-promotion, classing
ourselves among those who have privileges and rights above others.

Regardless of how legitimately we may lay claim to a position of
authority, or the "right" to lead, all such postures that claim prerogative
above others controvert Jesus' ministry. Though He held the highest
position in Heaven, He *"did not regard equality with God a thing to be
grasped, but emptied Himself."[35]* Regardless of one's position in this
discussion, we want to maintain the attitude of heart Jesus left us as an
example. How can we legitimately claim to know truth about any matter
of Scripture if we abandon His heart for His people?

---

[34]James 3:13   [35]Philippians 2:6-8

66

1 Timothy 3:1-13

> *"It is a trustworthy statement: if any man aspires to the office of overseer, it is a fine work he desires to do. An overseer, then, must be above reproach, the husband of one wife, temperate, prudent, respectable, hospitable, able to teach…"*
>
> ~ 1 Timothy 3:1-2

The final passage we'll examine in our study seems, at first glance, to settle the issue of *women-in-ministry-leadership* quite conclusively. By saying, *"if any man…,"* Paul seems to be restricting spiritual eldership to men. However, the indefinite pronoun translated *"man" (tis)* can just as easily mean *"any person."* As is often the case in English, the expression *"man"* often signifies *all people,* regardless of gender. Jesus used it when He said, *"Man does not live by bread alone…"[1]* Every child of God receives spiritual sustenance through God's word, and, by using *tis,* there is clearly no attempt to limit spiritual nourishment to men only.

In his two letters to Timothy, Paul utilizes *tis* twenty times, often in statements that refer to believers in general, and not exclusively to men. For instance, he speaks about *men (tis)* who *"teach strange doctrines"[2]* and *men (tis)* who *"stray from the truth."[3]* Similarly, *some (tis)* reject *"a good conscience"*—and suffer shipwrecked faith.[4] Paul says, *some (tis)* will *"fall away from the faith."[5]* Both men and women can, and do, fall away from the truth. The universality of *man (tis)* is further demonstrated when it is translated *"any woman"* later in his letter to Timothy:

> *"If any woman who is a believer has dependent widows, she must assist them and the church must not be burdened, so that it may assist those who are widows indeed."*
>
> ~ 1 Timothy 5:16

---

[1] Matthew 4:4   [3] 1 Timothy 1:6   [5] 1 Timothy 4:1
[2] 1 Timothy 1:3   [4] 1 Timothy 1:19

Would we ever teach that only men fall into the temptation of longing for money?[6] Are women free from the charge to compete *"according to the rules"?*[7] Obviously the answer is, "No." That is why I have never been troubled by the use of *man (tis)* when Paul encourages believers to aspire to spiritual leadership.

One Wife

Nevertheless, the text quickly presents us with an additional statement that, once again, seems to indicate elders must be men. Among the listed qualifications for eldership, we see the simple phrase, *"husband of one wife."* No woman can be a husband, so does that imply no woman can be an elder? Let's answer that question with another. Is it reasonable to imply that unmarried men are unqualified to be elders? A single man has no wife, so must all elders be married? Are single men restricted from ministry leadership?

That would seem rather unlikely based on the simple fact that Paul, himself, was unmarried. In fact, he advises people to remain single if they are able—so that they may give *"undistracted devotion to the Lord."*[8] It makes no sense to see *"husband of one wife"* as a prescription, a necessary life-circumstance for eldership. The issue for Paul is more likely one of self-control, someone who knows how to manage his life well. Interestingly, no other qualification for spiritual leadership found in this text is gender-specific.

> *...it seems more likely that "one wife" reflects a person's character, not their life-situation.*

Since the *"one wife"* trait is listed in the midst of several other character qualities that mark someone as a possible elder in the Church, it seems more likely that *"one wife"* reflects a person's character, not their life-situation. In an era when it was somewhat common for men to have more than one wife, Paul wants to caution Timothy away from appointing elders with several wives.

[6] 1 Timothy 6:9-10
[7] 2 Timothy 2:5
[8] 1 Corinthians 7:32-35

The emphasis, in my mind, is not on the necessity of being a married man, but of having only one spouse. Since women with more than one husband were unknown in those days, there would have been little need for Paul to mention monogamy as a key ingredient in a female leader's life. However, in a society rife with bigamy and polygamy by men, the issue was likely one that Timothy would encounter as he sought for overseers in his flock.

Deacons?

Verses 8 through 10 deal with *deacons (diakonos)* as opposed to *elders (episkopē)*. Neither of these leadership offices is defined precisely in the New Testament. Many church traditions see *deacons* as somehow less spiritual in their leadership role, so the qualifications for becoming a *deacon* are less stringent than those for *eldership*. Deacons handle practical, non-spiritual issues in church; *elders* see to more spiritual matters.

Historically, this differentiation comes from Acts 6 where Peter urges the selection of *"seven men of good reputation, full of the Spirit and of wisdom,"* who can be put in charge of food distribution.[9] There is no scriptural basis in that story for presuming that deacons only deal with logistics. In fact, two of the listed "deacons," Stephen and Philip, have profoundly spiritual ministries. Nowhere do we find these two offices set in a sort of leadership hierarchy. For all we know, deacons were *elders-in-training,* or simply individuals who were considered too young to be elders.

The ministry scope of deacons is very important—especially to those people who do not believe women can be spiritual leaders. They must define *deacons* as less spiritual than *elders*—and more involved in "helps" than in ministry leadership. Otherwise, verses 11 and 12 present a problem. Paul specifically shifts his discussion of qualifications for deacons from men to *women (gunē):*

> *"These men must also first be tested; then let them serve*
> *as deacons if they are beyond reproach. Women must*

---

[9] Acts 6:1-6

*likewise be dignified, not malicious gossips, but
temperate, faithful in all things."*

~ 1 Timothy 3:10-11

Obviously, Paul allows women to be deacons. Deacons were leaders of
some sort. A deacon was a recognized office for which men and women
had to be tested in character and proven over time. Men and women who
"served well as deacons" within their congregations gained *"high standing"*
and *"great confidence" (parrhēsia).*[10] Literally, they became *outspoken* with
frankness and confidence of speech! That hardly fits with the traditional
picture of deacons quietly mopping the floor or limiting their ministry
oversight to logistics, administration, hospitality and mercy ministries.
Deacons and deaconesses, men and women *"filled with the Holy Spirit,"*
spoke *"the word of God with boldness"* in the Early Church.[11]

Notice how parallel these verses about *deacons* are to those about *elders.*
We find, yet again, why the phrase *"husband of one wife"* cannot easily be
construed to mean that ministry leadership should be restricted to men.
After specifically describing qualities that ought to be modeled by *women-
in-ministry-leadership,* Paul repeats what he said earlier:

*"Deacons must be husbands of [only] one wife, and good
managers of their children and their own households."*

~ 1 Timothy 3:12

Paul simply recognizes what we all know to be true—that different
groups of people face different sorts of challenges and opportunities.
"One wife" is not proof that elders and deacons are gender-specific roles.
Rather, he is suggesting a gender-specific qualification for men who wish
to be elders or deacons.

Differences Not Restrictions

Admonitions, instructions and cautions given to one gender, as opposed
to another, simply acknowledge the unique opportunities, as well as

---

[10] 1 Timothy 3:13   [11] Acts 4:31

challenges, they have in living out the ways of God. According to Paul, older men ought to be *"temperate, dignified, sensible, sound in faith, in love, in perseverance;"* likewise, older women should be *"reverent in their behavior, not malicious gossips nor enslaved to much wine, teaching what is good."*[12] *Young women, young men* and *bond-slaves* each receive admonishments for how to live their lives in a way that *"adorns the doctrine of God our Savior in every respect."*[13]

> **No groups are excluded from living the way others are encouraged to live.**

No one would suggest, however, that older men needn't be *"reverent in their behavior"* simply because that admonition is expressly addressed to women! Biblical instruction is often specifically aimed at certain individuals and people-groups, but that instruction is not limited to those addressed. No groups are excluded from living the way others are encouraged to live.

Because the real-life contexts of different sorts of people are somewhat unique, God's word offers counsel to *young* and *old, slave* and *master, Jew* and *Gentile, man* and *woman.* Since we are all God's children (and He corrects those He loves), every category of people receives some caution and censure in the Bible. It was neither racist nor limiting for Paul to acknowledge one tendency among the Greeks (to *"search for wisdom"*) and another among the Jews (to *"seek for signs"*).[14]

Jesus addressed men's inclination to look lustfully at women, but His focus on men certainly didn't mean He was allowing women to lust after men; it's just that men and women tend to have different vulnerabilities. Humanity's carnal nature ever seeks its own convenience.

Our race is prone to setting ourselves above others.[15] The young want to throw off the yoke of their youth;[16] masters tend to treat their workers unjustly.[17] One race despises another; we prejudice our treatment of

---

[12]Titus 2:2-3

[13]Titus 2:4-10

[14]1 Corinthians 1:22

[15]Judges 17:6; Ecclesiastes 4:1-4; 9:3; 1 John 2:16

[16]Lamentations 3:27; Ephesians 6:1; 1 Peter 5:5

[17]Jeremiah 22:13; Malachi 3:5

> *Name any people-group in life, and you will find, in the word of God, corrective statements to refine their walk and strengthen their ministry effectiveness.*

people based on worldly standards.[18] A wife can lose respect for her own husband, just as a husband may fail to sacrifice himself for his own wife.[19] People who are being led sometimes rebel against leaders, and leaders sometimes lord over and take advantage of followers. [20]

Name any people-group in life, and you will find, in the word of God, corrective statements to refine their walk and strengthen their ministry effectiveness. We are clay vessels, broken in many places. We need strengthening. We must be shored up at vulnerable spots if we are going to carry everything God wants us to bring to others. The point is that neither *Greek nor Jew, old nor young, female nor male*[21] have less ministry opportunity simply because they are singled out for encouragement—or correction.

The life-course of each person varies from that of another, but we all find direction at the foot of the same Cross. Depending on numerous life-factors—not the least of which are age and gender—believers are

> *We are, in the world's eyes and in God's, priests and ministers of a New Covenant.*

brought into conformity with Christ from singular starting points and along different courses. No group has a fast-track. No group is granted dispensation that excuses them from character formation, simple obedience or spiritual instruction.

CONCLUSION

I believe it is neither biblical nor realistic to argue for ministry equality based on male-female sameness. Men and women are different from one another. God intended those differences, and He cannot be glorified by any attempt to blur the distinctions that enable us to fit together in

---

[18]James 2:1-9
[19]Ephesians 5:22, 25
[20]Numbers 12:1-3;Ezekiel 34:1-5; Hebrews 13:17; 1 Peter 5:2-3
[21]Galatians 3:28

partnership. But the differences between men and women are not restrictive in ministry.[22]

From the whole of God's Word, I see God's redemptive, restorative work in the world, and how He establishes believers as *"oaks of righteousness"* who repair *"the ruined cities, the desolations of many generations."*[23] Our collective destiny and ultimate calling as God's children, both male and female, is to be *"priests of the Lord...ministers of our God."*[24] We are, in the world's eyes and in God's, priests and ministers of a New Covenant. It has always struck me as incongruous for some members of the Church to disallow women the very designation that God and the nations approve.

[22]1 John 2:12-14
[23]Isaiah 61:3-4
[24]Isaiah 61:6

…But Among You It Will Be Different

by Jenifer A. Manginelli, MATS

The previous pages have laid out a scriptural basis for women participating in every aspect of ministry. Daniel Brown has now provided me the opportunity to close this article by speaking personally about my own wrestling with the issue and where the dust is settling for me.

My main concern regarding this whole issue is actually for the hearts of women who feel called to ministry. I'm concerned that as we debate the topic, we could lose sight of the real issues. What if, while we contend for freedom to minister in Jesus' kingdom, we in actuality sell out to a spirit of selfish entitlement that jeopardizes the very calling we long to have recognized? The stakes are high, because the enemy of our soul would love nothing better than to turn an area of freedom into something that stifles the gifts within us that Jesus intended to be a great blessing to *His Church*.

A Reflection

Not long after my husband Chris and I moved to Seattle to become lead pastors, I taught at our weekend services. Later that day Chris received an

email from a man who had been visiting and was deeply offended that
I had been allowed to speak from the pulpit. He laid out reasons for
why I was unqualified to handle God's word. Chris composed a
response in my defense, to inform him that I was actually well qualified
to teach. But then, after further reflection, we decided to delete it and
send a simple response, asking forgiveness for making him feel that
God's word was being dishonored in any way. That was the furthest
thing from our intention.

We acknowledged that we came from different traditions with
theological differences—this issue of "women teaching" being one of
them. Then we communicated our chief desires: 1) for people to
understand and experience the love of Jesus; and, 2) for us all to be
obedient to the call of God on each of our lives.

But, before I begin, I feel it is important to acknowledge a couple of
things:

1. When it comes to the issue at hand—whether or not women have
    freedom to participate in every function and aspect of ministry—I
    would be remiss not to acknowledge that there is a wealth of
    scholarship on both sides of the issue.[1] The fact that well-studied and
    sincere followers of Jesus have come to differing conclusions speaks to
    the complexity of the witness in Scripture.

2. While I believe Scripture teaches that gender is of no issue when
    it comes to gifting and calling, the vast majority of people I have
    met (both men and women) who feel that women should not hold
    places of spiritual influence and authority are motivated by a
    sincere reverence for God's word. They want to take the text at face
    value and not manipulate it to say what is politically correct. I
    honor that.

Note: All scriptures referenced in this chapter, unless otherwise noted, are taken from
the *New Living Translation*.

[1] See the bibliography at the end of this article for some definitive theological works
that support both of the primary understandings of the relationship between men
and women: *complementarian* and *egalitarian*.

A SIMPLE PREMISE

The life and example of Jesus must shape our expectations of calling and ministry—nothing more, nothing less. This matter of whether or not, according to Scripture, women are called to teach is messy—not only theologically, but also in stewarding an attitude and expectation for ministry. There is a slippery slope between *privilege* and *entitlement*. In trying to navigate calling and ministry, I have stumbled down that slope more times than I would like to admit. Proverbs 4:23 says, *"Guard your heart above all else, for it determines the course of your life."* This is such wisdom for ministry.

> *I am more and more convinced that this question of whether or not women should be in ministry belongs to a larger conversation...the conversation about who will be the greatest.*

I am more and more convinced that this question of whether or not women should be in ministry leadership belongs to a larger conversation—the conversation we have all had in our heads at one time or another—the conversation about who will be the greatest. Jesus said in Matthew 20:25-28, *"You know that the rulers in this world lord it over their people, and officials flaunt their authority over those under them. But among you it will be different. Whoever wants to be a leader among you must become your slave. For even the Son of Man came not to be served but to serve others and give his life as a ransom for many."*[2]

Jesus' disciples are getting a little ahead of themselves, imagining how things would turn out when Jesus came into His kingdom—specifically, where they would sit. Jesus' response is incredulous, *"You don't know what you are asking! Are you able to drink from the bitter cup of suffering I am about to drink?"*[3] In so many words, Jesus was saying, "You are asking the wrong question. You are daydreaming about what is in this for you, showing that you don't really understand the cost of My mission in this world."

We, like the first disciples, follow Jesus to the best of our ability with sincere intentions. But we also have other desires and catch ourselves

[2]Matthew 20:25-28; cf. Mark 10:43-45; Luke 22:24-27   [3]Mark 10:35-38

daydreaming about our own places of honor. The longer His disciples walk with Him, though, they figure out that He is headed for the Cross; and, that if they (and we) are really going to follow Him, that means, in one sense or another, they (and we) are headed there too. And along the way, as we learn of the way of Jesus, our imaginings about what kind of glory and honor is in this for us fall away.

A DIFFERENT ECONOMY

In response to the disciples' question, Jesus makes the most of a teaching opportunity by drawing a contrast between the way things operate in earthly kingdoms and the way of His kingdom. What is to be the defining characteristic of Jesus' Church? What is it that our lives are to be marked by?

> *As believers, our identity lies not in the categories of this present age...but rather in Christ as the distinguishing mark of every believer.*

While it is certainly true that the Church should be a strong advocate for social justice, this advocacy is evidence of a deeper, remarkable freedom from egocentrism. In other words, advocacy within Christianity is not akin with insistence on rights, but rather the preferential treatment of others motivated by love. The two could not be more different from one another.

We find a certain tension reflected in Scripture about equality—and the resulting benefits. On the one hand, Paul makes very clear that what Christ has done on the Cross has changed everything. As believers, our identity lies not in the categories of this present age (male, female, slave, free, rich, poor), but rather in Christ as the distinguishing mark of every believer.[4] Naturally, this understanding is expected to overflow into our everyday lifestyles and result in giving preferential treatment to one another.[5] Yet, for Paul, the emphasis is on living in a Christ-honoring way in the midst of our social situation, rather than insisting upon an elevated

---

[4]Galatians 5:6   [5]Philippians 2:3-4

status because of our new identity. This certainly appears to be true within the context of cultural categories.

In Ephesians 6:5-9, Paul exhorts slaves to serve their masters with the same sincerity as they serve Christ. He then goes on to say that their motivation is to go beyond simply pleasing their masters, to a deeper motivation of pleasing Christ. In turn, he calls masters to treat their slaves justly and to remember that they themselves have a Master in Heaven.

SOCIAL RELATIONSHIPS

What are we to infer from Paul's comments here in Ephesians about the validity of social relationships? Paul's instructions to slaves and masters immediately follow his instructions concerning children honoring their parents. While the child-parent relationship is certainly grounded in Scripture, the slave-master relationship seems, at the very least, questionable in light of kingdom values. Here Paul reflects a similar approach to Jesus in that while he did not directly challenge a cultural distinction, he did value people individually in a way that impacted them profoundly and testified to the radically different value system of the kingdom of Heaven. In a sense, Jesus and Paul advocated change from the inside out.

While Paul's approach here seems reasonable with regard to social situations, there remains the question of what Paul's expectations were within the Church. How are Christians to behave when both parties involved have a new value system? Paul exhorts slaves, *"Those who have believing masters must not be disrespectful to them on the ground that they are members of the church; rather they must serve them all the more, since those who benefit by their service are believers and beloved."*[6] So it would seem that even within the Church, Paul calls for an attitude of humility on the part of the underprivileged. But what about those within the Church who occupy positions of authority?

Paul's letter to Philemon speaks precisely to this issue. In this very brief book we catch a glimpse of Paul's heart for his new converts to recognize

---

[6]1 Timothy 6:2 New Revised Standard Version.

just how radical their new situation in Christ is. Paul asks that Philemon's spiritual understanding of Onesimus' value would transcend his cultural rights to Onesimus as his slave.

Two things are significant from these passages. First, within the confines of cultural distinctions, Paul expects Christians—both slaves and masters—to live as unto the Lord. He addresses both the underprivileged and the privileged to operate within their social framework on the basis of their values in Christ. Second, he calls on Philemon, the privileged, to act *beyond* his social rights and embrace Onesimus as a brother rather than as a slave.[7] Paul calls the socially privileged to use their power to affect the situation of the underprivileged. He likewise tells slaves of believing masters to respect and submit to them. However, Paul does not instruct Onesimus to contend for his value as a believer before his master.

WOMEN AND MINISTRY

Paul's approach to social distinctions in Ephesians and Philemon is consistent with his instructions concerning women and ministry. Christians have been perplexed as to exactly what Paul's stance was regarding *women-in-ministry-leadership.* On the one hand, there is evidence that Priscilla had a prominent teaching ministry within the Church and that the women greeted in Paul's letters also held positions of influence.[8] On the other hand, scholars have wrestled with the sharp words in 1 Timothy 2:12 regarding women who had apparently assumed leadership, *"I permit no woman to teach or to have authority over a man; she is to keep silent."*[9]

Scholars have speculated as to whether in making this statement, a timeless universal principle was being mandated, or simply a timely command to out-of-order women in Ephesus. What prompted this command—was it the fact that *women* were demanding authority and

---

[7]Philemon 1:10-12
[8]Acts 18:24-26; Romans 16:1-7

[9]1 Timothy 2:12 New International Version

80

creating disorder in the Church, or was it the *disorder* itself that elicited such a response? I tend to think that it was the latter.[10]

What message do these passages, when set alongside one another, hold for people who feel that they have been overlooked and underestimated in ministry? First, if we are going to follow the example of Jesus, we have no card of entitlement to play. If anyone could have played that card, it was Jesus. Yet, He set His glory aside to serve us, for our benefit. Paul sets Jesus as the ultimate example and personification of humility:

> *"Though he was God, he did not think of equality with God as something to cling to. Instead, he gave up his divine privileges; he took the humble position of a slave and was born as a human being. When he appeared in human form, he humbled himself in obedience to God and died a criminal's death on a cross."*
>
> ~ Philippians 2:6-8

If we are going to follow in the footsteps of Jesus, we must minister out of a profound sense of obedience and sacrifice. Earlier in Philippians Paul reminds his readers, *"For you have been given not only the privilege of trusting in Christ but also the privilege of suffering for him."*[11] Jesus was underestimated, misunderstood, considered a threat, and questioned about His motives. Servants are not greater than their master, so it should not surprise us that if we follow in the way of Jesus, we too will encounter suffering. Yet, when we suffer for His sake, it is a holy privilege. If the intention of our hearts is to walk in humility and obedience, then we can trust God for where the chips fall. Certainly He is worthy to be trusted with this.

If the intention of our hearts is to walk in humility and obedience, then we can trust God for where the chips fall.

---

[10]For a detailed discussion about what Paul's letters teach regarding women and ministry, I highly recommend Cambridge New Testament Scholar Philip B. Payne's book, *Man and Woman, One in Christ: An Exegetical and Theological Study of Paul's Letters*. Grand Rapids: Zondervan, 2009.

[11]Philippians 1:29

We spend most of our lives trying to become something—something meaningful, maybe even something impressive. Much of the time we mistakenly imagine that our life is all about us, when, in fact, nothing could be further from the truth. Jesus talked a lot about losing everything to gain one thing—the thing that truly matters. When we encounter Jesus, we trade everything we were going to make of our lives in and of ourselves for a life we never dreamed we would live—a life where we are free to live beyond ourselves, beyond our pain, beyond our insecurities and beyond our selfishness.

The process is messy and it takes a lifetime. Along the way, we discover that becoming like Jesus is not as glamorous as we imagined it to be. Letting go of what we were going to be of our own merit does not happen easily. And, often what has been laid to rest once has a way of reappearing. And so, we go through the whole process again and again on increasingly deeper levels.

> *He entrusts His sheep to faithful shepherds who are guided by genuine concern for His sheep.*

UNLIKELY MINISTERS

Additionally, there is biblical precedent for God using unlikely and unqualified people to unfold His kingdom purposes. Those of us who feel overlooked and underprivileged should take heart in this. God uses people who are more concerned with accomplishing His purposes than are enamored with themselves. He entrusts His sheep to faithful shepherds who are guided by genuine concern for His sheep. Inevitably, feeling the need to promote ourselves and impress leads to insensitivity towards the needs of others and a clouding of God's plans and purposes by our own agenda. So, tragically, by being preoccupied with ourselves, we unknowingly disqualify ourselves from the work of ministry.

Conversely, being willing to be overlooked and misunderstood actually speaks of a remarkable sense of identity. It is far better to wait for God to make room for gifts He has given than to insist on rights we feel have been withheld. Self-promotion is profoundly unbecoming. I have often asked myself the question, "Why does it matter to me that I am recognized in this situation?" When I feel overlooked and underestimated, I want to believe that I am outraged because of my desire to wash people's feet. But if I am really honest, I am outraged because somewhere deep inside, I still have thoughts about who will be the greatest.

I think we all want to be dead to ourselves, but few of us are interested in the process of dying—because dying hurts and it requires long-suffering. Yet, how can we read the New Testament and expect anything different from a life of devotion to Jesus? It is right there in the text over and over again that we must pick up our cross and follow Him—that he who seeks to save his life will lose it, but he who loses his life for His sake will find it.[12]

I have wondered if this preoccupation with greatness among believers is peculiar to the Western world. In Maslow's hierarchy of needs, the top level is self-actualization—a level only reached when the immediate needs of survival are not overshadowing it.[13] I doubt followers of Christ who experience persecution struggle with thinking about greatness. Perhaps it is the comfort and wealth in which we pursue Christ that makes us think that we can have our cake and eat it too—that we can have our own career and agenda and also follow Jesus. More than once I have felt the Holy Spirit speak to my heart asking the question, *"Jenifer, which is it going to be: your way or My way? Because if you really want to follow Me, you have to deny yourself."*

While it is not wrong to hunger for encouragement, I am coming to realize that basing the significance and value of serving on how it is regarded by others proves to be a faulty gauge for what it means to serve in God's kingdom. Therefore, in some sense, it is a blessing to be overlooked and underestimated, because it calls us to die to ourselves and allow Christ to be formed in us. He is our motivation. He is our reward. He is our identity.

---

[12]Matthew 10:38
[13]A.H. Maslow, *A Theory of Human Motivation,* Psychological Review 50(4)(1943):370-96.

I'm convinced that throughout our human experience we, at one time or another, sit in both chairs—"privileged" and "underprivileged." The question is, how have we stewarded each of those situations? Our propensity is towards self-exaltation and self-preservation. Therefore, we must constantly check ourselves when we feel overlooked and underappreciated, and likewise when we feel a sense of entitlement or superiority.

> *If God has placed me in a position of influence, then I have the opportunity and even the responsibility of...making room for the gifts of others.*

We have to fight to have the mind of Christ—to operate, not according to the patterns of this world, but by the often counter-intuitive economy of the kingdom of Heaven. This necessitates taking inventory of our hearts and owning when we are being small and petty, so that we can ask for pure motivation and perspective. The following are things I remind myself of from the perspective of each "chair."

WHEN I FEEL ENTITLED. . .

(1) "Steward your influence"

If God has placed me in a position of influence, then I have the opportunity and even the responsibility of advocating—of making room for the gifts of others. It is a sobering thing to be entrusted with something by Jesus, especially the very people He gave His life for. In the parable of the talents, Jesus is disappointed and frustrated with the servant who buried His own talents; I shudder to think of how He would feel about one servant burying the talents of another.[14] Paul exhorts the Philippians:

> *"Don't be selfish; don't try and impress others. Be humble, thinking of others as better than yourselves. Don't look out only for your own interests, but take an interest in others too. You must have the same attitude that Christ Jesus had."*
>
> ~Philippians 2:3-5

---

[14]Matthew 25:24-30; Luke 19:20-27

(2) "Don't forget your story"

I have to be leery of a heart attitude that leans in the direction of, "How dare they—do they know who I am?" I can't forget my own story because we all have the same story: that while we were yet sinners, Christ died for us. We are recipients of a most lavish grace that we must extend to others. In 1 Corinthians 1:26-29, Paul addresses believers in Corinth who were bragging about who had baptized them. He tells them to take a good hard look at who they were before Christ, and to think twice about that in which they are going to place their security. He writes:

> *"Remember, dear brothers and sisters, that few of you were wise in the world's eyes or powerful or wealthy when God called you. Instead, God chose things the world considers foolish in order to shame those who think they are wise. And He chose things that are powerless to shame those who are powerful. God chose things despised by the world, things counted as nothing at all, and used them to bring to nothing what the world considers important. As a result, no one can ever boast in the presence of God."*

(3) "Remember to whom the glory belongs"

A sobering question I ask myself is, "Can God trust me with His glory?" One thing I like about the Apostle Paul is that he never forgot who he was and who he was becoming. Others may have spoken more eloquently, but he made no apology for who he was not and who Christ was in him. He wasn't confused about who should receive the glory. So deep-seated was his security in Christ that he would say:

> *"So now I am glad to boast about my weaknesses, so that the power of Christ can work through me. That's why I take pleasure in my weaknesses, and the insult, hardship, persecutions, and troubles that I suffer for Christ. For when I am weak, then I am strong."*
>
> ~ 2 Corinthians 12:9-10

When I Feel Overlooked. . .

(1) "Measure yourself by your own standards"

What have I done with the influence that God has given me? Have I
stewarded it to my benefit only, or am I

*What have I done
with the influence
that God has
given me?*

constantly looking for someone else I can
make room for at the table? It is easy to find
fault with those who have influence beyond
mine, but I have to make sure that I don't
myself personify the very attitude towards
leadership that I am bearing up under. Jesus taught that a spiritual
principle of His Kingdom is *"those who are faithful with little, will be entrusted
with much."*[15]

(2) "Don't make room for yourself"

Advocating for myself doesn't work. An advocate is, by definition, "one who
pleads on another's behalf." I constantly have to remind myself that my part
in accomplishing ministry is to pick up my cross and follow Jesus. It is Jesus'
responsibility to take the loaves and fish that I offer Him and feed the
multitudes. His disciples didn't think much of the boy's offering of loaves
and fish, but who could argue with what it became in the Master's hands?

(3) "Be hard to offend"

Jesus has called me to be hard to offend. This is something my husband
reminds me of often, not only with his words, but by the way he responds
to people. When I feel like turning the other cheek is too high of a price,
I need to remember the price that was paid for my own sin. And, when
I turn the other cheek, I am freed from the tremendous weight of
embitterment. It also takes the teeth out of accusations. There is nothing
more frustrating than someone who is humble and selfless when we are
in the mood for a fight—when we want to have a conversation about
who is the greatest. In Colossians 3:12-14, Paul writes:

---

[15]Luke 16:10

"Since God chose you to be the holy people he loves, you must clothe yourselves with tenderhearted mercy, kindness, humility, gentleness, and patience. Make allowance for each other's faults, and forgive anyone who offends you. Remember, the Lord forgave you, so you must forgive others. Above all, clothe yourselves with love, which binds us all together in perfect harmony."

SO, WHERE DOES THE DUST SETTLE?

I think a good rule of thumb is to focus on what it is about the gospel that is painfully clear, and allow that to inform matters that are debated. Regardless of how we interpret specific New Testament texts regarding women and ministry, the universal call of all Christians is to lay down our lives, pick up our cross and follow Jesus. If we preoccupy ourselves with this, it will be hard for us to be too far amiss. And, while we may be voiceless to the Church at large, it is sobering to consider that we are the only ones who will give an account to our Master for how we have stewarded our own hearts. It is so much easier when we feel overlooked to quit and become cynical. But let's go the distance; let's remain faithful.

Further, if leadership in Jesus' kingdom is really washing people's feet, then what are we arguing about? We call our own bluff when we insist on our rights. In Jesus' economy, the issue isn't whether or not we have entitlement—because either way, the call is to humble ourselves and be poured out for those to whom we minister.

"After washing their feet, he put on his robe again and sat down and asked, 'Do you understand what I was doing? You call me 'Teacher' and 'Lord,' and you are right, because that's what I am. And since I, your Lord and Teacher, have washed your feet, you ought to wash each other's feet. I have given you an example to follow. Do as I have done to you.'"

~John 13:12-15

The life and example of Jesus must shape our expectations of calling and ministry—nothing more, nothing less.

Recommended Reading

Following are four outstanding works from differing perspectives:

1. Cambridge New Testament Scholar Philip B. Payne's detailed exegetical study based on decades of research interacts with all of the scholarly works that follow. He entered his research from a complementarian point of view and was persuaded otherwise through his studies. *Man and Woman, One in Christ: An Exegetical and Theological Study of Paul's Letters.* Grand Rapids: Zondervan, 2009.

2. Eldon Jay Epp (from a theologically liberal perspective, a penetrating and extraordinarily insightful analysis of Rom 16:7). *Junia: The First Woman Apostle.* Minneapolis: Fortress, 2005.

3. Kevin Giles (an Australian Anglican from a broadly evangelical perspective wrote this brief but very insightful overview of the issues). *Women & Their Ministry: a case for equal ministries in the church today.* East Malvern, Victoria, Australia: Dove Communications, 1977.

4. Millard J. Erickson (a Baptist theologian with mature thought and solid philosophical grounding). *Who's Tampering with the Trinity? An Assessment of the Subordination Debate.* Grand Rapids: Kregel, 2009.

The most widely read anthology from the complementarian viewpoint:

- Piper, John and Wayne Gruden, eds. *Recovering Biblical Manhood and Womanhood: A Response to Evangelical Feminism.* Wheaton, Illinois: Crossway, 1991.

The most widely read anthology from the egalitarian viewpoint:

- Pierce, Ronald W. and Groothuis, Rebecca Merrill. *Discovering Biblical Equality: Complementarity Without Hierarchy.* Downers Grove, Illinois: InterVarsity Press, 2004.

Co-Author Bios

KELLY TSHIBAKA co-pastors Mount Vernon Foursquare Fellowship in Alexandria, VA (just outside D.C.) with her husband, Niki. She is a mom to three children and works as an attorney for the federal government. She has a heart for discipling, leadership development, healing ministry, church multiplication, and encouraging and equipping women in ministry. She also likes to sing (though she isn't that talented...), write, scrapbook, and laugh!

JENIFER MANGINELLI and her husband Chris serve as lead pastors of Mill Creek Foursquare just north of Seattle, WA. It is her greatest privilege to mother Emma, Eli and Luke. She is also an adjunct professor at LIFE Pacific College, specializing in Biblical Languages and Old Testament Theology. She has a life-long love of learning and teaching . . . anything involved with people realizing their God-given potential. In the odd event that she finds spare time, she spends it flipping through a Pottery Barn magazine and dreaming of her next trip to London.

ABOUT COMMENDED TO THE WORD
The Resource Ministry of Daniel A. Brown, PhD

Our name, **"Commended to The Word,"** comes from Acts 20:32. Paul commends spiritual leaders "to God and to the word of His grace which is able to build you up and to give you the [kingdom] inheritance…" Our materials focus on increasing believers' maturity, ministry and discernment.

CTW is a non-profit resource ministry that has grown out of Daniel Brown's extensive relationships in Europe, Asia, and South America. Today Daniel travels widely to mentor pastors and young leaders, and to distribute a wealth of ministry resources.

SEMINARS BY DANIEL BROWN

Daniel provides workshops and conferences to church leaders worldwide. His presentations are keenly biblical, and his insights about discipleship, church leadership and spirit-empowered ministry, coupled with his unassuming manner, make him an approachable and engaging speaker. Daniel's seminar topics include:

- "Next Steps" for You and Your Church
- Deliverance Ministry
- Prophets, Prophecy and Prophesying in the Church
- Discovering Ministry Gift-Mixes
- Family Life Seminars
- Bible Study Workshops

Whether your group is large or small, you can schedule leadership workshops by contacting seminars@ctw.coastlands.org. For more information visit our website, ctw.coastlands.org and click on the "Seminars" tab.

CONTACT COMMENDED TO THE WORD

Email resources@ctw.coastlands.org

Phone 831.688.2568

Follow us on Facebook [f] and Twitter [t]

Visit Our Website ctw.coastlands.org

Our Bible-based materials focus on encouraging not only your own personal growth, but also on developing your ministry to others. Come search our vast library of pastoral resources:

- Downloadable MP3s of Audio Series

- Podcasts of Daniel's Messages

- A Huge Library of Audio and Video Sermons

- Articles and Outlines

- "Open Letters" from Daniel's Pastoral Experience

When you visit the CTW online store, you'll also find books, audio CDs and DVDs available to you at cost.

DOWNLOADABLE MATERIALS ARE FREE AT
CTW.COASTLANDS.ORG

IF YOU ENJOYED THIS STUDY, YOU MAY BE INTERESTED IN DANIEL BROWN'S BEST-SELLING BOOK...

Enjoying Your Journey with God

Book $10.00

A totally practical, non-religious guide to understanding your Christian faith, this book offers 14 topical Bible studies compiled into one volume. Believers both young and seasoned will build their faith in these interactive chapters designed for personal or small-group study:

- Being Loved Without End
- Being Recovered From Evil
- Experiencing Grace
- Loving and Forgiving Others
- Being Baptized With the Spirit
- And more

Disfruta tu diario vivir con Dios

Book $10.00

Now available entirely in Spanish, Dr. Daniel Brown's innovative Bible study has become a popular Christian guidebook throughout the worldwide Hispanic community. Its personable, non-religious style and deep insight make it accessible to believers of all ages, and its practical wisdom for applying the principles of faith make it unique in the Spanish-speaking church. There are 14 chapters designed as topical Bible studies suitable for home groups or personal growth.

Cries Against the Shepherds

Booklet $3.00

Spiritual authority and abuse are not easy topics to discuss. Dr. Daniel Brown bravely tackles this delicate subject with sensitivity and depth, exploring the motives behind unwarranted slander against spiritual shepherds. Some of the topics he covers in this booklet are:

- Recognizing Your Own Clay Feet

- The Difference Between Control and Godly Authority

- How to Assess an Accusation

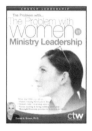

The Problem With...The Problem With Women in Ministry Leadership

2 Audio CDs + free MP3 Download $5.00

In this companion audio presentation, Daniel discusses the theme of women in church leadership with fresh focus and a clear explanation of the "problem" passages in 1 Corinthians 11, 14 and 1 Timothy. These scriptures lead many sincere believers to think that only men should be spiritual leaders, but does the whole of scripture support this idea? Find out what the Bible says about...

- Women teaching in the Church

- Meaningful leadership positions for women in the Church

- Women having authority over a man